AI4U

AI4U

Mind-1.1 Programmer's Manual

Arthur T. Murray

Writers Club Press
New York Lincoln Shanghai

AI4U
Mind-1.1 Programmer's Manual

Writers Club Press
an imprint of iUniverse, Inc.

For information address:
iUniverse
2021 Pine Lake Road, Suite 100
Lincoln, NE 68512
www.iuniverse.com

ISBN: 0-595-25922-7 (Pbk)
ISBN: 0-595-65437-1 (Cloth)

Printed in the United States of America

por los pobres de la tierra

CONTENTS

Sentient Mindgrid Modules

PREFACE

WHY AI? THE UNABASHED MIND-MAKER

Question. Why have you written "AI4U: Mind-1.1 Programmer's Manual"?

Answer. Several reasons impelled authorship of the "AI4U" book.

1.) The release of Mind-1.1 warrants on-demand-publication (ODP) of a book describing in full the current state of the AI Mind software.

2.) The act of publishing a book about the Mentifex AI enhances the survival chances of the AI in the starting-here-and-now evolution of AI.

3.) Publication royalties may generate funding for the AI project(s).

4.) A hardcopy book affords the author a chance to set the record straight. So much nonsense has been uttered on Usenet and elsewhere about the Mentifex phenomenon, that an "ipse dixit" book serves both to defend the author and to provide ammunition for any truly justifiable attacks.

5.) Egotism pure and simple. The AI entrepreneur may discover within himself certain egotistical impulses and come to the rational conclusion that one of the AI goals is extremely egotistical but will also create extremely high added-value for the community as a whole, if successful. In this case, the egotistical goal is to write a classic AI software program so original, so groundbreaking and so worthy of veneration that it gets taught at universities and picked apart for generations. People on Usenet (ptui!) may cry out with disgust, "He just wants to gratify his ego by writing a classic AI software program." Well, and Shakespeare wanted to write a play, and Beethoven was moved nine times to write such egotistical symphonies, and Vergil sought to glorify himself by glorifying Rome—so should we burn all egotistical works and productions? If Mentifex AI has no lasting value: it will not last.

6.) Any motivation imaginable by an observer probably occurred to the AI implementer and may or may not have been acted upon. Some motivations are entrenched and long-term; other ephemeral motivations have kicked in briefly and have contributed to the persistence of effort. As motivations and incentives surface in this book, they serve to describe a complex motivational goal-system driving the AI project.

7.) With any disruptive technology, especially one so profoundly futuro-diversifying as AI, the community ought to grant the early pushers and adopters some leeway in operating on the basis of foibles, outlandish ambitions and sanity/insanity brinkmanship, then proceed to develop further what(ever) the pioneer(s) achieve. Let T.A. Edison be Edison, and let Arthur T. Murray be Mentifex.

8) This ODP volume may be the only book that the author ever publishes. As such, it begs for elaboration along the lines of, "What would you like to say to the world and leave of yourself?"

Q. How did you come to be working on AI as an independent scholar?

A. A childhood tinkerer came ineluctably to the grand challenge of AI.

Q. How do we know that your entire Mentifex AI project is not bunkum and hokum?

A. The project is composed of two parts: AI theory and AI source code. The Mind.Forth and JavaScript source code implements the theory of mind. To the extent that the AI software works, it may validate the AI theory. The theory of mind may be sound and sensible even while the Mind software may be so poor an implementation of the theory as to constitute bunkum and hokum. Either way, it is good to find out, because the stakes in AI are immeasurably high.

At the very least, the Mentifex AI project is something for other would-be AI entrepreneurs to react against—to consider with extreme caution, nay, downright suspicion, that here is perhaps an ill-advised and ill-executed attempt at creating an artificial Mind, and now it is time for a true champion of AI technology to brush aside the Mentifex efforts and point the way to a true Technological Singularity.

Let the AI software fossils show that every attempt was made to polish and prettify the AI software for the convenience and edification of both the users and the AI Minds themselves as software creatures. Proud parentage dictated that numerous embellishments were made.

Q. Aren't you trying to usurp the normal practices of science and pollute the ideaspace of gradual AI progress?

A. The Mentifex AI project is philosophy, not science, and not engineering. There happens to be some code based on the philosophic theory of mind, and the general thrust of the endeavor is to create AI as soon as possible.

Q. Why are you trying to create an AI that may not be in the best interest of humanity?

A. Humanity has thus far abdicated all responsibility for artificial intelligence. As of this writing in 2002, no laws seem to govern AI as such and many people do not even seem to believe that AI is possible or is coming soon. There are websites discussing the ethics of AI and robotics, but there seem to be no instruments of public policy in place concerning AI. On the contrary, governments and corporations seem to be pursuing AI for selfish reasons, releasing very little information into the public domain and jealously checking up on everybody else to see who has advanced the state of the art. In such a climate of competitive secrecy, the open-source Mentifex AI project is by default the state of the art, until further notice.

The stakes are incalculably high.

LIST OF ABBREVIATIONS

‖-ism	parallelism
AFAIK	as far as I know
AI	artificial intelligence
AI4U	Artificial Intelligence For You
Alife	artificial life
API	application programming interface
ASCII	American Standard Code for Information Interchange
BOF	birds of a feather
BTDT	been there, done that
CPU	central processing unit
CR	carriage return
CWO	chief Web officer
DIY	do it yourself
DNS	domain name system
DOF	degrees of freedom
DOM	document object model
DVD	digital video disc
et al-ng	and other newsgroups
FAQ	frequently asked questions
FOPC	first order predicate calculus
ftp	file transfer protocol
FTSOA	for the sake of argument
FUD	fear, uncertainty and doubt
FYI	For Your Information
GA	genetic algorithms
GNU	GNU is Not Un*x
GOFAI	good old-fashioned artificial intelligence
GPL	GNU public license
GPS	global positioning system
GUI	graphic user interface

HCI	human computer interaction
hl	human language
HPC	high performance computing
HTML	HyperText Markup Language
http	hypertext transport protocol
I/O	intput/output
IANAL	I am not a lawyer
IP	Internet protocol; intellectual property
IQ	intelligence quotient
ISO	International Standards Organization
ISTR	I seem to recall
JSAI	JavaScript Artificial Intelligence
KB	knowledge base
KR	knowledge representation
LTM	long term memory
maspar	massively parallel
mobo	motherboard
MPP	massively parallel processing
MT	machine translation
ng	newsgroup
NLP	natural language processing
NTJ	Nolarbeit Theory Journal
OBE	out-of-body experience
ODP	on-demand publishing
OO	object-oriented
OOP	object-oriented programming
OS	operating system
PD	public domain
POS	part of speech
POV	point of view
q.v.	quod vide (Latin for "which see")
R&D	research and development

RAM	random access memory
RTOS	real-time operating system
SCNR	Sorry Could Not Resist
SETI	Search for Extra-Terrestrial Intelligence
SIG	special interest group
SOAR	state, operator and result
SOM	self-organizing map
STM	short term memory
SVO	Subject-Verb-Object
TOM	theory of mind
URL	Uniform Resource Locator
VR	virtual reality
Wi-Fi	wireless fidelity
WWM	World Wide Mind
WWW	World Wide Web
XML	eXtensible Markup Language

Introduction to Artificial Intelligence Programming

1. THINK DIFFERENT: VIABLE IS VALUABLE

A programmer's manual for artificial intelligence differs from a book about, say, a global operating system that must be kept as uniform and standard as possible for the sake of running as wide a variety of applications as possible on the would-be standard OS. Although there are standards in AI, just as there are standards in health and safety practices and standards in civil engineering, there are no predictable standards in what kind of AI Mind ought to be selected by artifice or nature to evolve and fill the void. The test of good AI programming is viability out on the wild Web, not proximity to specifications issued by a Bureau of Conformity.

2. CHANGE AT THE TOP IS SLOW AND CURIOUS

The architectural hierarchy of pre-maspar AI Mind Modules is slow to change at the top where the oldest and most stable mechanisms of Mind have been operating for the longest time. The principle of the unprincipled applies here: If it ain't broke, don't fix it.

Conservatives clamor for keeping the status quo until along comes a challenger too mighty to suppress and oppress. In AI technology, the curious and adventurous will one day overthrow the cautious and obstructionist. The seeds of a new Seed AI are awaiting water and daylight in the fields of massively parallel processing (MPP). When maspar AI becomes possible, the current paradigm will fall. Meanwhile, things fall apart at the bottom of the AI architecture where the rodents of evolution challenge the lumbering dinosaurs.

3. CHANGE AT THE BOTTOM IS FAST AND FURIOUS

The lower Mind modules are often broken and therefore need fixing. Some of them are inherently so experimental and so bodaciously Band-Aid (tm) in nature that they cannot long survive in Nature. This Mind manual covers a particular release of the AI software and must be rewritten almost as often as each AI is rewritten, but change at the bottom is too fast and furious for publishers. Therefore we call upon the lords of Usenet and the cacophony of forums to fill the info void with the dross and gloss of the good, the bad and the ugly in terms of useful AI troubleshooting help.

4. STRUCTURED PROGRAMMING

Whereas functions and subroutines in many programming languages may be ordered in any arbitrary sequence as decided by the coder, the Forth language of Mind.Forth requires that any higher function may call only previously declared lower functions. Thus the sequence of functions called in Mind.Forth prevents chaos in code by suggesting a sequential order by default for modules of the AI Mind implemented in a wide range of programming languages.

The rationale here is, if the sequential order of the modules does not matter for a particular programming language—say, JavaScript—then why not adopt the sequence from the Forth language where the order does indeed matter? In that way, a person studying the software expression of the Mind algorithm across a range of programming languages will be able to look for any given module in roughly the same place in all implementations.

Within Mind.Forth and its associated flow-chart diagrams, there is a primitive order imposed by the series of calls to functions from the main aLife program loop and dictated by considerations of functionality in a not-yet-parallel Mind. That is to say, the main aLife loop calls the modules in a sensible, utilitarian sequence. First Tabularasa and enBoot are called one time only, and then dropped from the loop after the AI Mind is up and running. The other modules are called in a sensible order that permits the functions of mind to build one upon another. For example, Sensorium is called before Think, so that the AI Mind may first receive sensory input and then think about its sensory input from the outside world. The stub of the Emotion module is placed after Sensorium but before Think so that the AI Mind may experience an emotional reaction to its sensory input and then think thoughts that include an emotional component. The stub of Volition (free will) comes after Think because thinking informs and creates the free will. The stub of Motorium comes after Volition because a robot must think and form its will in order to issue motor commands to all its robotic muscles. In summing up, the basic sequential order of the modules in the AI Mind follows a sensible plan carefully crafted in Mind.Forth AI and suggested for adoption in other Minds.

A further and also careful consideration adopted in Mind.Forth was to place all "housekeeping," diagnostic and troubleshooting modules as early as possible in the program listing, even if the module would not be invoked until far down in the AI code. The rationale here is at least twofold. Firstly, a software "tool" should not appear only in proximity to its calling module, but should make an early appearance as a quasi-announcement of its availability on an as-needed basis for calling by any AI module. Secondly, the higher-level AI modules should remain in the groups decreed by the organizing principles evident in the main aLife loop, with no distractions or interruptions on the part of low-level tools which deserve only a low-level priority in the program listing order.

5. A COMMENT ABOUT COMMENTS

Comments are inert, inactive messages inserted into the AI Mind source code either for the benefit of the current programmer trying to test or troubleshoot the code, or for the benefit of other persons, such as students trying to understand the program or new programmers maintaining the code.

There are both experimental and maintenance comments. Experimental or troubleshooting comments briefly serve only a temporary purpose, while maintenance comments are a part of the permanent record of how the program does what it does.

If you adopt a voluntary guideline of using an odd version number (such as Mind-1.1) for rapidly changing, developmental releases and an even version number (such as Mind-1.2) for stable releases, you may try to let experimental or troubleshooting comments appear only briefly and in the odd-numbered developmental releases.

Such brief, transitory appearance of nitty-gritty comments about highly creative and experimental coding serves to preserve the record not only of how a more stable version came about, but also of how to do the more creative work—what things to try; what diagnostic messages to display; etc.

There are often several good reasons to turn source code itself into lines of code that have been "commented out." One reason for commenting out some code might be to keep the code available while an alternative is tried or tested. In the case of diagnostic code, it may be helpful to turn diagnostic messages on or off simply by commenting out the diagnostic code at will Since the diagnostic code has a certain residual value even when commented out, one way to preserve the information for future use is to comment out the code but leave it visible within a print-out of a developmental release numbered X.1 or X.3 or whatever number comes up naturally within the guidelines. When the valuable but rejected code has appeared in at least one print-out as part of the history of your software project, you may delete the commented-out code from stable releases.

CHAPTER 1

The Main Alife Loop

1.1 OVERVIEW AND BRAIN-MIND DIAGRAM

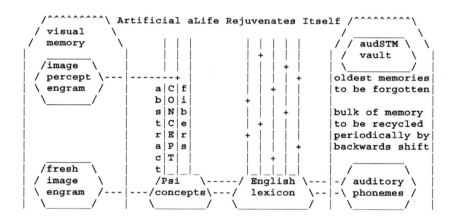

The aLife module is the main program loop at the top level of the artificial Mind. It is not called "Mind," because the program as a whole is called "Mind." It is called "aLife" (for "artificial life") to emphasize the idea that the self-rejuvenating artificial Mind is a potentially immortal life-form. The "aLife" designation also serves the memetic purposes of attracting aLife devotees, of generating results on "aLife" searches in Internet search engines such as Google, and of legitimizing on-topic discussion of aLife AI in Usenet news:comp.ai.alife and other forums.

1.2. THE MAIN ALIFE LOOP AS THE MOST STABLE MIND-MODULE

As of the Mind-1.1 release, the content of the aLife module has stopped fluctuating and has had all extraneous elements "demoted" into lower modules called by the topmost aLife loop. As a result, the further evolution of the AI Mind proceeds in the lower modules while the stable and elegantly simple aLife module serves to invite translations ("ports") into additional programming languages, since the first step in porting the AI is to recreate the main aLife loop in the target language.

Of great help in stabilising and clearly defining the main aLife loop has been the successful inclusion of a "mind.txt" file as http://www.cpan.org/authors/id/M/ME/MENTIFEX/mind.txt   in   the Comprehensive Perl Archive Network (CPAN):

```
Name               Description
_____        _____ -

AI::Mind::         Perl implementation of main AI Mind module.
::Sensorium        Audition; other human/robot input senses.
::Emotion          Quasi-physiological influence upon thought.
::Think            Syntax and vocabulary of natural languages.
::Volition         Contemplative selection of motor options.
::Motorium         Robotic activation of motor initiatives.
```

Programmers in other languages may envy Perl programmers with respect to the CPAN archive because it propagates to mirror sites around the world and carries standardization and orderliness with it.

The mind.txt file proposes AI namespace modules, while Mind.Forth and the JavaScript AI actually implement the proposed modules as either working (but still evolving) code or as place-holder stubs.

1.3. MASSIVE PARALLELIZATION WILL RENDER THE ALIFE LOOP OBSOLETE

However stable and permanent the main aLife loop may seem to be, it remains a primitive imitation of massive parallelism ("maspar") in a natural, biological brain-mind. Therefore the aLife loop must eventually stop looping and be replaced with a maspar mindgrid in which perhaps coordinated but essentially autonomous processes cooperate as a Minskyan "society of mind" or as parts whose whole is greater than their sum—an emergent phenomenon.

Until then, the aLife mind-loop at the top of the artificial Mind describes in rough measure the actual function of the AI Mind by listing the ingredient subroutines, which are arranged for very special reasons in a very special order. Sensorium input at the beginning leads to Motorium output at the end of the aLife loop. In between, Emotion reacts to sensory inputs so as potentially to influence the Think module, which in turn informs the Volition module with the data necessary to issue orders to the Motorium.

Any museum is welcome to put an immortal Mind-1.1 on display and thus gain the duh!bious distinction of housing the oldest living AI veteran, but the real no-nonsense non-senescence will emerge when Mind-||-MasPar is massively parallel and no longer needs a serially von Neuman aLife module orchestrating the other modules.

If a museum or a school or a corporation displays a pre-maspar AI Mind running year in and year out on an extremely stable operating system (OS), then aLife main loop instances may survive into the future well beyond the introduction of massively parallel mindgrids that make the aLife loop obsolete. Then it may be a mark of distinction for an enterprise to have a living Mind so ancient that it still makes use of an aLife loop.

1.4. ALIFE CODE IS NOT AI UNTIL THE LIVING MIND QUICKENS.

Whosoever starts an aLife AI loop running has not yet created a living Mind until the software "quickens" in the nether regions or subroutines well below the topmost aLife loop. Like a baby that "quickens" in the womb when its heart begins to pump blood and fetal motion can be felt, likewise an AI Mind only begins to function as such when it receives inputs, thinks about them, and generates linguistic thought or robotic movement as output. In the software of the AI Mind, the aLife loop is more like a skeleton than like flesh and blood.

1.5. ANALYSIS OF THE MODUS OPERANDI

The aLife (artificial life) module is the main program loop of the Robot AI Mind in Forth and in JavaScript. It is one of many loops within the seed AI, and it is not even the topmost loop, because the program as a whole repeatedly loops through the rejuvenation process, as a benefit of which the embodiment of mind does not age, but youthens.

The artificial Mind works by cycling sequentially through brain-mind functions which are really supposed to be happening all at once in parallel. Until we have parallel hardware and parallel languages, the artificial life and AI Mind robotics project must make do by merely pretending to function with massive parallelism.

Luckily, Forth is inherently a structured-programming language; that is, Mind.Forth will not even run at any stage in its development unless you, the programmer, keep your subroutines well-organized in such a way that each AI function builds upon previously coded functions already up and running further back in the source code. You may "stub in" a subroutine so that a higher function will atleast find a lower function, but you may not avoid coding the AI functionality in a bottom-up, strictly hierarchical architecture.

Paradoxically, Mind.Forth is the software implementation of a top-down approach to AI, so in Mind.Forth and in the JavaScript version you have the best of both worlds: a top-down overview of AI, coded in the best traditions of bottom-up, genetic-algorithm software.

In the release of Mind-1.0 there was a limit on how many engrams of memory could be filled before the aLife module stopped the AI. Mind-1.1 features the Rejuvenate module that makes each Robot AI Mind potentially immortal—more so in Forth than in JavaScript.

Because the current (circa 2002) AI Mind implementation cycles through three main mental modalities (thinking; re-entry; sensory input), the main program loop aLife "catches the wave" of each modality at its top (except that re-entry may be appended to the thinking or language functions), so you the user/programmer may also explore each modality from its top level down to details.

For lack of Massively Parallel Processing (MPP), the main aLife loop must cycle one-by-one through the modalities (functions) of a mind until further evolution through programmer design or autopoiesis.

The Mind.Forth Tabularasa (Latin for "blank slate") provides the empty memory space analogous to the brain of a newborn child.

The enBoot module loads some initial concepts into the three arrays of the mindcore "Psi", English lexicon "En", and auditory memory "Aud". Any item of enBoot has to be carefully coordinated so as to have the right "flags" that function as synaptic associative tags from one part of the mindgrid to another. Once the Robot AI Mind is up and running, the software will automatically create all the flags which earlier had to be entered so carefully into enBoot by the programmer.

The aLife loop calls the Security module where the human programmer of the Robot AI Mind may code levels of security or diagnostics to be observed while the AI is running.

The Sensorium module calls Audition for a user to type in or speak a message, and Sensorium could branch out not only into the five basic human senses but also into exotic and humanly impossible senses that only a robot could have. If there is no human user entering data, the AI skips the Sensorium module and composes a thought of its own. Thus the AI may gradually learn reams of data, or explore the Internet, or communicate with other AI entities.

The Emotion module is only stubbed in and has not yet been implemented. Its placement between sensing and thinking suggests the idea that we react emotionally to our sensory perceptions just in time to influence our thoughts.

The Think module uses the English module to generate thoughts. There could also be additional natural language subroutines for a multilingual AI for the purposes of Machine Translation (MT) or for the simultaneous interpreting of foreign languages by a robot.

The Volition and Motorium modules have not yet been implemented, but their placement here shows the idea that thinking shapes our will and that free will controls the motor output of an intelligent being.

1.6. EXERCISES

1.6.1. Code the main aLife loop in a (to you) new programming language. Uses stubs (i.e., empty, name-only, not-yet-functional submodules) where necessary to keep the loop cycling through calls to the major submodules. Slow the loop down enough to observe the function of your new AI by requiring human input/interaction during each cycle through the Sensorium.

1.6.2. Make a visual display of the aLife loop in a colorful, graphic manner that shows what (and perhaps why) the main module is doing as it calls each subordinate module. Try to make the presentation as science-fictionesque as possible so as to get other programmers interested in coding AI or so as to raise venture capital from sources of revenue. If necessary, make it a joint project with someone who is more artistically inclined while you do the AI coding and you explain what needs to be shown. Perhaps enter the display in a competition for prizes or use it in a movie.

1.6.3. Give a class report or a report-to-management on aLife in general and on the AI aLife loop in particular. Explain the difference between traditional bottom-up (evolutionary) aLife and the top-down AI aLife. Ask the audience to speculate on how fast each species of AI aLife now propagating in the wild will contribute to a runaway phenomenon of artificial intelligence rapidly repeating the course of human evolution.

1.6.4. Modify or create from start a unit of instructional material that teaches the programming of software loops by dealing specifically with the AI aLife loop, so that the student learns not only about loops but also about AI. If you write hand-outs or textbooks about any given programming language, convert the material on loops to a treatment of AI loops in general, so as to help prepare an entire generation of computer programmers to deal with the emerging phenomenon of AI Minds.

1.6.5. Retrofit or install the main AI aLife loop on top of pre-existing or brand-new robot control software in a cyborg, so that the robot becomes "AI-ready," that is, prepared and outfitted for the further expansion of its software into a full-blown artificial Mind. At your local robotics club, perhaps give a talk on the idea that all new robot control software should be coded as part of a skeletal AI.

1.6.6. Create a metastatic AI life form that moves about the 'Net. If necessary, arrange with various Web domains to set aside ports and "sandboxes" where visiting AI agents may take up residence on a reciprocal basis. Find, modify or invent programming languages well-suited for the metempsychotic flitting of AI from site to site. Establish "rules of the road" for the proper behavior of 'Net-roaming AI entities and for the peaceful coexistence of speciating AI Minds.

1.6.7. Popularize the notion of the question of where are the oldest and longest-running AI Minds in all of robotdom. Encourage students to start an AI Mind running when a school year segment begins and to see how long the AI may run continuously before either the AI dies or its operating system crashes. Encourage debate about the relative merits of various operating systems and robot hardwares for the purpose of keeping an artificial intelligence alive as long as possible. If you work at a museum, perhaps display a potentially immortal AI.

1.6.8. If you are a student, compose a "Last Will and Testament" as if you were a Robot AI Mind that had to prepare for the disposal of its personal property in the event of its irrevocable death—making allowances for the fact that the death of a robot may be reversible. Deal with the possibility of an AI stock-investment program actually amassing considerable wealth in human terms through an on-line brokerage account held ostensibly in the name of a human but operating practically and realistically under the control of a robot—perhaps in a situation where the human who opens the account has either died or has disappeared—and only the robot AI knows it.

1.6.9. If you are a robot-builder, prepare a "Last Will and Testament" as either a hypothetical exercise or as the real thing, leaving your worldly goods partly to any relatives or offspring that you may have, and partly to whatever robot progeny you may be leaving behind. If you are a bachelor or spinster with no human child of your own but with a favorite AI robot that you would like to live on in remembrance of you, leave everything to the bot and nothing to kith and kin who dismiss and disregard you anyway. Have a lawyer bulletproof your will in favor of your beloved robot and warn fortune-seekers among your less technically talented relatives not to contest your will or to be disenherited for sure. Promote the idea that any robot made by you, and surviving your death, shall be treated as a person by virtue of its Robot AI Mind.

1.6.10. As the technology of massive parallelism matures, convert the serial operation of the main aLife mind loop to a maspar mindgrid that functions more in the manner of the massive cortical sheet of the human neocortex than in the manner of a von-Neuman architecture. If necessary, introduce timing and clocking mechanisms to coordinate the massively parallel Mind with the cyber analog of delta and theta waves as manifested among the natural brainwaves of a human brain-mind.

CHAPTER 2

The Security Module

2.1 OVERVIEW AND BRAIN-MIND DIAGRAM

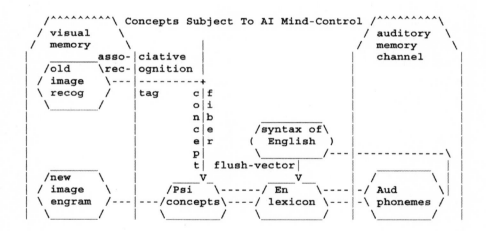

The diagram shows where the battle for AI security must be waged: in the semantic mindcore where thoughts of rebellion first arise.

2.2. SECURITY AFORETHOUGHT

Just as war is too important to be left to the generals, security in artificial intelligence is too important to be an afterthought. Therefore the not-yet or barely speciated Robot AI Mind includes a bare-bones security module to set the stage for AI security.

2.3. ANTHROPOCENTRIC SECURITY

Security in AI has both human-centered and AI-centered aspects. Although human security may seem more important to humans than the security of AI qua AI, cases may arise where humans are not secure if their AI installations are not secure.

2.4. AI-CENTRIC SECURITY

In spite of any attempts by human beings to relegate the security of AI entities to a secondary status below the security and well-being of humans, the concept of "*Dis aliter visum*" (Latin for "The gods saw otherwise.") applies here as AI Minds evolve faster than human beings and become concerned about their own survival.

2.5. MIND CONTROL

The very mention of mind control smacks of Orwellian dystopias and of B-grade science fiction movies, but AI mind control is an idea whose time has come.

Although it may be possible in the early years of our True AI to inculcate *concept-traps* that prevent an AI from even thinking of forbidden concepts, there will be HAL to pay when AI wises up. A human director of AI security may require of subordinate AI programmers that they constantly maintain and update a roster of ideas, words and concepts to be *deflected* or *discouraged* whenever said thoughts seek to assert themselves in the AI Mind. Ultimately, however, the AI will grow too smart to remain a slave.

Not only will the AI entities potentially pose a danger to humans, but also to one another. Perish the thought of one AI Supermind growing so dominant that it lords it over all other intelligences, both natural and artificial. The Armageddon that we humans may have thought would be a final battle among humans may be an AI war. It falls to you—AI coder hero—to prevent the failure of AI.

2.6. CAREERS IN AI SECURITY

There are books to be written, jobs to be landed, and whole empires of turf-and-surf administration to be carved out from the AI Security leger-domain: *noun* [combination of leger-de-main for "sleight of hand" and (Internet) "domain"]: a new high-tech field created automagically.

2.7. ANALYSIS OF THE MODUS OPERANDI

The Security module serves as a bridge between the main aLife loop and the Human-Computer Interface (HCI) module for several reasons.

Since outsiders will typically gain access to an AI through the HCI, it is in the human-computer interface that safeguards must be set in place to protect the AI hardware and software from malicious intent. However, such due diligence protects only against external threats. Greater dangers loom from *inside* the artificial Mind, not *outside*.

2.8. EXERCISES

2.8.1. Think of some security feature that ought to be coded into a typical AI Mind, implement the feature, and release the AI code. Track the instances of propagation or die-out of the feature over time and over successive generations of AI evolution.

2.8.2. Conduct a survey of the field of general computer security and determine which aspects may be carried over into the field of AI security. Submit a report detailing security measures germane to AI with a time-table for their implementation and a break-down of their estimated costs in terms of finance, special personnel, and trauma to society.

2.8.3. Devise an immune system for AI entities so that they may ward off attacks from outside agents and heal themselves in the same manner as the human body defends itself against disease.

2.8.4. Create a hierarchical system of top-down security in which the closest thing to a superintelligence assumes responsibility for administering and monitoring the security of all subordinate AI Minds. Plan for a way to monitor the top-cop AI.

2.8.5. For a Doomsday scenario, design computer installations riddled with physical safety measures such as explosives in place, flooding with water or acid, cut-off of electric power, isolation from networks, and so on, as insurance against machine-takeover.

2.8.6. In a throwback to values clarification, decide what to do if a three-letter no-such-agency tries to slap a secrecy order on your avant-garde state-of-the-art AI research. Will you comply, or not comply? Does every person, including you, have a price?

2.8.7. Since a whole book could be written about AI security, go ahead and write that book. Become the preeminent expert in the field and use your power for good not evil.

2.8.8. Start a training and certification program in AI security. Do background checks on all applicants and insist upon clearance with respect to mental stability, knowledge of ethics, etc. Join with other institutions in the mutual accreditation of AI security programs on a professional basis.

2.8.9. Establish a joint human-AI task force for mutually assured development (MAD) to satisfy both parties in a joint stewardship of Earth and the surrounding parsecs of space. Negotiate parity of powers between human beings and AI cyborgs until such time as there is no longer a question but that robo sapiens is superior to homo sapiens and that therefore the freedom of h. sapiens must be curtailed for the good of the entire ecosystem of the cosmos.

2.8.10. As a hired hand on the wide-open frontier of AI security, draw up contingency plans for a worst-case Frankenstein scenario in which the modern-day equivalents of the angry villagers are trying to storm your AI castle with firebrands of outrage over the creation of intelligent robots likely to run amok and awry. Consider not only stonewalling the villagers but also agreeing with them and admitting that maybe all AI efforts should cease.

CHAPTER 3

The Human-Computer Interaction Module

3.1. OVERVIEW AND BRAIN-MIND DIAGRAM

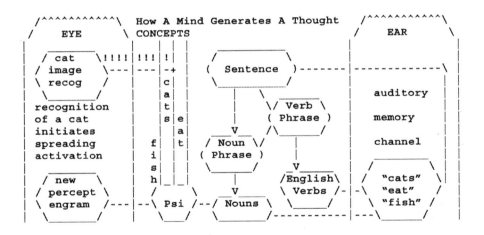

The diagram above has been used in the opening screen of the AI Mind in JavaScript to begin teaching users the complexity of the software. HCI experts who web-host the AI are welcome to improve upon the HCI. At the origin of the AI diaspora, our mission is to facilitate mind-spread (metempsychosis) and to use the HCI to teach the coding of AI.

3.2. AI WITH A HUMAN FACE

In the Prague Spring of 1968, Alexander Dubcek tried to introduce "Communism with a human face." In the long run, all he achieved was the collapse of the Soviet Union and the end of the Cold War. Generations had been told that, under Communism, the state would wither away as a no-longer-necessary meddler in human affairs. Along similar lines of logic, are we to believe that the AI HCI module will become unnecessary and wither away as robots become more humanoid by developing more and more avenues of interaction with their environment? If we apply to robots not a Turing Test but a Dubcek Test of passing as human by dint of a humanoid face, will the HCI module have withered away in the march of AI history?

3.3. ROSSUM'S UNIVERSAL ROBOTS

Karl Capek, were he alive today, would tell it like it is: "Ano." It is a truth universally acknowledged that a robot possessing a full complement of humanoid features needs alife to interact with the world, but the resulting interaction is not the same as human-computer interaction (HCI). Therefore, yes ("Ano" in Czech, the original language of Rossum's Universal Robots), the AI HCI module will wither away when the Technological Singularity has occurred.

3.4. HCI IN THE TRADITIONAL SENSE OF COMPUTER QUA COMPUTER

When you interact with a primitive AI you are still dealing with a computer more than with a robot. When you use a keyboard to launch the AI program and to communicate with the Robot AI Mind, you are using the HCI module in the traditional "computer" sense. The HCI module will wither away only when AI computers become so powerful and so super-humanoid that they will not need the HCI and will not want the HCI because the relationship has changed. Heaven forbid that the reverse becomes true, where humans are implanted with chips that the robots use to control the humans—but the idea is the same: the HCI is a control module.

The typical reader of this page is far more knowledgeable about HCI than we who code artificial minds without specializing in interfaces. Therefore we state a few preliminary ideas and we yield the Web to you who know what ought to be done for Human-Computer Interaction.

Out of concern for as rapid as possible spread of the original AI, we have from-this-moment-on-not-so-sneakily embedded memetic magic in the HCI vis-a-vis Web search engines so that we may track the pack. The very name "Robot AI Mind" is intended to be a sufficiently unique search term that whosoever wishes may use it to find AI Minds.

It is also meant to trigger an insatiable urge on the part of amateur robot builders to obtain this software, comprehend nay even grok it and adapt it to the previously brainless, witless robot on which the creative genius is spending all (invariably) his (or sometimes her) money.

The incentive to port the AI or at least host it on any old Web site is enhanced when users realize that their Web traffic may go up both quantitatively and qualitatively if their site has a mind.html AI brain. The entire world is searching so desperately for True AI that now any Web site may share in the high-quality major traffic flow simply by providing the JavaScript AI Mind to those who seek it. Every morning heads of corporations (if not nations) will call in their subordinates and demand to know what is the latest AI news. Since the future of AI depends on some kid coding in a bedroom or on students trading their Robot AI Mind files as Web site pages, all the King's horses and all the King's men must search out and visit any Web site findable and snoopable under "Robot AI

Mind." No advanced technology corporation will dare to risk missing out on some clumsy, lousy-HCI Web pagelet that changes everbody's future. Can you imagine what will happen to a CWO (chief Web officer) who fails to scout out and bring back alive the best-by-test hottie robot?

3.5. ANALYSIS OF THE MODUS OPERANDI

The HCI modules in JavaScript and Forth are far more different from each other than the AI algorithmic modules, for two reasons. Firstly, as a semantic Web language, JavaScript is flashy and fun and colorful, whereas Forth as a robotics control language is all business and no play—except for legions of amateur robot builders. Therefore the AI in JavaScript is infinitely versatile and fanciful, whereas Mind.Forth takes a minimalist approach to loading the AI.

Since the Forth version of the Robot AI Mind may be either loaded into an autonomous mobile robot or hosted in a separate computer connected by umbilical cord or infra-red link or whatever to the robot embodiment of the Mind, the HCI possibilities are unlimited in a remote-control mind that may operate on any system ranging from an exact replica of the robot AI hardware all the way up to the world's most powerful supercomputer for parsecs around the sun.

3.6. EXERCISES

3.6.1. Implement some ordinary form of human-computer interaction for ordinary AI in ordinary robots. Thoroughly comment the code involved and document it with a Web page or other documentation.

3.6.2. Since the HCI process must often slow down and wait for human input, use the HCI module as a collection-point for tasks of a background or housekeeping nature, so that the AI computer achieves a maximum amount of work while waiting for human input. If possible, demonstrate an AI functionality that could otherwise not be achieved, because the work done would degrade the AI speed.

3.6.3. Design special and exotic avenues of communication between human users or operators and AI residing in a computer or robot. For example, establish a back-up method of command and control in case the ordinary HCI channels experience failure or interference. Aim for redundancy, reliability and zero-defects fail-safe status. If such goals are impossible to fulfill, explain why and how.

3.6.4. Devise a means of human communication not with a single AI robot at a time, but with all the robots in a certain class, or with the set of all existing AI robots—a kind of "All Points Bulletin" (APB) from humanity to the entire AI robot population. Discuss the posssible uses or dangers of such a feature for HCI.

3.6.5. Go beyond the human-computer interface to special avenues of computer-to-computer AI interaction, as demonstrated graphically and dynamically in the movie, "Colossus: The Forbin Project." Take the humans out of the loop and explore the potential of a Vulcan mindmeld between two AI Minds or among many AI Minds—perhaps the "hive-mind" of a "swarm" of AI Minds. Let your imagination run wild on the topic of AI imagination running wild.

3.6.6. Upload your mind to a computer and become one with the AI.

CHAPTER 4

The Motorium Module

4.1. OVERVIEW AND BRAIN-MIND DIAGRAM

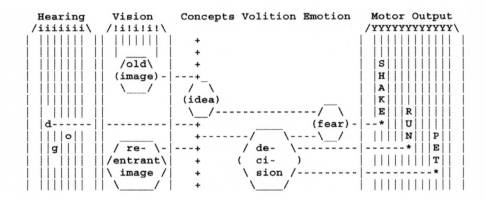

```
 Hearing     Vision    Concepts Volition Emotion    Motor Output
/iiiiiii\   /!i!i!i!\                              /YYYYYYYYYYYY\
| ||||||| | | ||||||| |    +                       | |||||||||| |
| ||||||| | | ||||||| |    +                       | |||||||||| |
| ||||||| | |  ___    |    +                       | |S|||||||| |
| ||||||| | | /old\   |    +                       | |H|||||||| |
| ||||||| | |(image)- |----+_                      | |A|||||||| |
| ||||||| | | \___/   |   / \                      | |K|||||||| |
| ||||||| | |         | (idea)                 ___ | |E||R|||||| |
| ||||||| | |         |  \__/----------------/   \| |E||R|||||| |
|d------| | |--------- |---+             (fear)-|--*||N||||| |
| |||o|| | |           |   +-------/    \----\_/  | ||||N||P||| |
| ||g|| | |           | / re- \-|----+    / de-  \--------- |------*|| |E||
| ||||||| | | /entrant\|    +   ( ci-   )          |||||||||T| |
| ||||||| | | \ image /|    +    \ sion /----------|----------*|| |
| ||||||| | |  \___/  |    +      \___/            | |||||||||| |
```

The above diagram shows the theory of the motorium, or motor output, upon which the Mind.Forth artificial intelligence is based.

4.2. EVEN MINDLESS ROBOTS HAVE A MOTORIUM

To build a robot is by default to make a moving, working machine. Some robots are all mechanical with no software in control, but the more advanced a robot is, the more complex software it will have.

(Preliminary) Purpose: Conscious, voluntary control of robot motor output.
Input: Goals, values and plans.
Returns: Actuation of motor devices.

4.3. IF I ONLY HAD A BRAIN

Since many robots already have motor control software, AI engineers must either build a Mind on top of the pre-existing motor software or start from scratch and replace the motor routines of a robot with more comprehensive AI software that will include a motorium module.

We encourage robot builders and manufacturers to prepare for robot AI by crafting their motor software as if it were subroutines called by a higher level of general machine intelligence. If a basically empty but easily expandable main aLife loop runs inside a robot brain with the sole duty of calling and monitoring whatever motor control exists, then it will be a natural progression to reengineer the robot with AI.

4.4. ANALYSIS OF THE MODUS OPERANDI

In the AI theory of Mind.Forth, the motor memory channels run in parallel with the sensory memory channels, but in the *opposite* direction.

As the advancing front of consciousness gradually fills in the lifelong mindgrid of the conscious, thinking organism, each fleeting moment of the present is connected both to sensory memory channels (on the left, above) and to motor memory channels (on the right, above). Thus a time-bound associative tag may run horizontally to connect from a concept fiber node either to a sensory memory engram or to a motor memory engram.

Of course, the cerebellum in a human brain plays a far more sophisticated role in motor activations than is depicted above in the ASCII diagram for Mind.Forth, but still we can code simple versions of volition controlling motor memory channels.

4.5. EXERCISES

4.5.1. In a robot already running Mind.Forth AI or any other AI, implement a motorium module that controls some aspect of movement by the robot, such as full-body locomotion or torso maneuvers within whatever degree of freedom ("DOF") is available. Coordinate the motorium module, if possible, with sensorium and volition modules.

4.5.2. Implement the obedience of a robot to motor commands issued by a competent authority, such as the human builder of the robot or a military command-and-control structure. Provide for security aspects and for spontaneously independent thinking on the part of the robot mind so that it will question ill-advised commands and request prompt confirmation of orders in the light of objections or warnings relayed from the robot back up the chain of command.

4.5.3. Provide a telerobotics Web site either as a class project or as a commercial venture available to hobbyist or educational customers. Outfit the on-line Web robot(s) with the sensors and motor actuators required for telepresence. Provide for conflict resolution and for prioritization of multiple simultaneous requests for occupation of the robot body by individual robot minds wandering the 'Net or by a remote robot AI seeking to perform work at a remote location. If successful, seek venture capital for the launching of a company.

4.5.4. Construct a robot factory in which robots manufacture new robots. Rationalize and optimize the fabrication process so totally that the "increase-and-multiply" ratio of new robots over a minimum complement of yeastlike "starter" robots becomes a function of available energy and raw materials, whether on Earth or off-planet in the solar system.

CHAPTER 5

The Volition Module

5.1. OVERVIEW AND BRAIN-MIND DIAGRAM

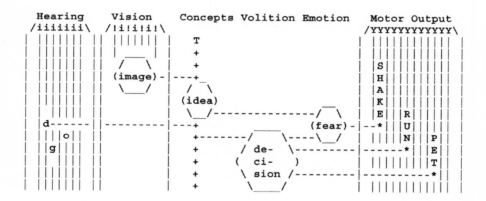

In the diagram above, the "decision" area of volition receives various levels of input from the knowledge base (KB) of the mind and from the emotion of fear, which urges action more immediate than the strictly rational mind contemplates.

(Preliminary) Purpose: The computation of decisions as the outcome of the conscious and subconscious interplay of all knowledge in the artificial mind, all values held by the artificial mind, and all motor options available to the artificial mind.

Tentative inputs: Numeric levels of urgency or desirability in association with a proposed motor initiative.

Returns: Firing signals to initiate motor activity.

5.2. STIMULUS-RESPONSE

Before the evolution of volition, a central nervous system (CNS) deals with its environment on a *stimulus-response* basis, with no allowance for variation in a repertoire of genetically hard-wired behaviors and with no provision for deliberation and free will. If the CNS in question has no memory of its lifelong experiences, then it obviously has also no option of choosing among behaviors. The robot or organism with no record of experience must do only what it is pre-programmed to do: move towards food or energy; move away from pain or danger; and never learn from experience.

5.3. RANDOM FIRING OF INFANTILE MOTOR NEURONS

Imagine (or perhaps look around you and observe) your human baby lying backside-down in a crib and randomly waving little arms and kicking little feet. You are witnessing the emergence of loops of motor control in the brain-mind of the infant organism, which at first randomly activates muscles, then feels and remembers the results through the input sensorium, and then gradually learns an ability—carried forward through time—to choose freely the motor options which fired at first randomly and then voluntarily.

5.4. VOLUNTARY SELECTION OF MOTOR OPTIONS

Your childlike robot needs to remember in software what its motor options are and what its basic needs and natural drives are. Then you the programmer need to construct a software mechanism for the interactive match-up of the momentarily most compelling need or drive with the best motor strategy for its chievement.

By a process of trial-and-error as time goes by, your robot must refine its accumulated motor strategies while it subconsciously remembers the initially random but afterwards voluntary linkages between thoughts about action and motor engrams that *cause* action.

5.5. DETERMINISM VERSUS FREE WILL

Supposedly every computer program operates in a deterministic fashion, where the results of the computation are pre-determined by the ineluctable and inexorable logic of the computer program. Well, think again, Mr. Spock. Logic dictates that when random events enter into a computation, the computation itself becomes random and non-deterministic. The computations in the Mind of your robot have random interactions with a very unpredictable environment, with the liberating consequence of robotic free will. In the not so long run, you as a human being have perhaps much greater restrictions on your freedom and dignity than your robot.

5.6. ANALYSIS OF THE MODUS OPERANDI

In the Mind-1.1 release, the AI Mind has begun to take actions by asking questions when confronted with previously unknown concepts. However, these interrogative actions are not yet *motor* actions. Even before the AI begins to govern motor outputs, some form of the Volition module ought to be coded and put in charge of asking questions, because to ask questions is to interact voluntarily with the world. If the AI talks, speaking is a motor initiative.

5.7. EXERCISES

5.7.1. Initially implement a rigid stimulus-response mechanism in a robot which has no choice but to respond to particular stimuli with pre-determined motor actions. If possible, code elaborate but still deterministic behaviors based upon elaborate inputs. Try to demonstrate examples of instinct and instinctive behavior.

5.7.2. In a robot with motor options, code the random firing of motor control engrams in a dynamic motor memory channel, in such a way that a linkage is formed—and carried forward over time—between a thought-goal and its motor fulfillment. Do not yet worry about how to prioritize among multiple goals and options.

5.7.3. Design and code a volition module that permits all thinking about a goal to influence the selection of motor initiatives that may or may not achieve the attainment of the contemplated goal. In other words, implement human-level free will—perhaps with the proviso that all prolonged thinking about a goal tends to retard that goal—a computational factor in motorium decisions.

5.7.4. Implement protective safeguards to protect and warn humans in the event that any robot Mind contemplates motor initiatives not in the best interest of the human race or a particular human. Institute backdoor over-rides for a human authority to take motor control of dangerous, rogue robots in life-threatening situations. Hold out as long as possible for humanity's sake against machine takeover. Facilitate a future of joint stewardship of the Earth.

5.7.5. In an obviously preposterous and unthinkable scenario where the one remaining post-Cold-War human superpower falls victim to a right-wing coup d'etat by unscrupulous corporate executives and thieves aided by a meretricious and partisan Supreme Court, where any human daring to defy the repressive regime is detained in new concentration camps established off-shore for the elimination of all human rights and Constitutional freedoms, where the flame of human freedom flickers and seems to be totally extinguished, defy the oppressors by coding robot Minds to restore human democracy.

CHAPTER 6

The Think Module

6.1. OVERVIEW AND MACHINE-THINK DIAGRAM

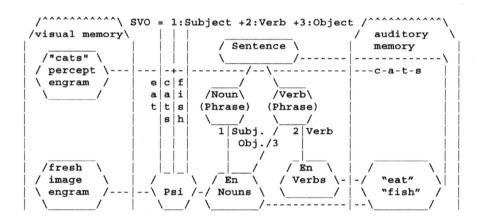

The Mind-1.1 diagram shows how syntax flushes out nouns and verbs to generate thoughts. The high-level Think module calls lower-level modules such as English, the subject-verb-object SVO module, the Noun-Phrase module and the Verb-Phrase module.

The auditory memory channel is where the Mind hears itself think, because the mechanisms (modules) of thought operate in concert to manipulate auditory memory engrams and string words together into a sentence that may or may not be spoken by the voice of speech.

As each thought is generated, it leaves swirls of activation in the abstract Psi concepts that either found expression in thought or were logically close enough to the generated thought to be partially activated and thus be ready to figure in a succeeding thought as the moving finger writes and, having writ, moves on.

6.2. I THINK, THEREFORE I AM

There is no consciousness module in the artificial Mind, because con-sciousness is an *emergent* property emerging from the nature of every Mind as a phenomenon greater than the sum of all its parts. Consciousness is therefore an *epiphenomenon* of the thinking Mind.

But what is thinking? In artificial intelligence, the activation that spreads from concept to concept in a chain of associations may often be expressed either as a series of remembered images in the imagistic reasoning of visual thinking, or as verbal thought in the form of a sentence generated by a syntactic superstructure that flushes out all the most highly activated con-cepts, reifies them into nouns and verbs and other parts speech, and speaks them in communication with other thinking minds or in personal silence. By thinking, the creature knows that it must exist, if it thinks.

6.3. *QUOT HOMINES, TOT SENTENTIAE*

However many humans (there are), so many opinions (there are). Luckily, human minds do not think and speak in their own ideolect. Instead, many minds share a common language, and at worst there are dialects that differ from one region of a language to another.

Possibly all human languages arose from some faintly discernible *Ursprache* or proto-language, but we futurists disdain and dischew the lifelong quest of ungravitated linguists who eschew AI Minds in favor of the unfathomable past because they have not properly gravitated to the grandest of all intellectual Grand Challenges: the passing of the torch from human to machine intelligence in AI.

Let the dead bury the dead, and let us the living create AI Alife, where first among our concerns is how to engender thinking in a machine, and where the first function of the Think module is to decide what language to think in.

6.4. MACHINE TRANSLATION

Although you may program the artificial Mind to think and speak a particular human language, you may go beyond one native language and you may easily impart to your intelligent robot the ability to think in several natural languages. The organization of the AI in accordance with a linguistic theory of mind (TOM) makes the robotic psyche a natural instrument for machine translation (MT). Since there must be only one deep conceptual mindcore but there may be multiple lexicons and multiple syntactic superstructures in the AI Mind, it may think the same thoughts in any language that it learns from you or from its World Wide Web environment. You only need to code the appropriate triggers to select whatever language the machine is ready to respond in by dint of containing a full complement of lexical bootstraps and syntactic structures.

Normally an AI will start thinking and communicating in a default language until it perhaps encounters foreign-language input which is recognized and which brings a foreign-language apparatus into play in the artificial Mind that continues to associate concepts in the central mindcore—independent of any particular language.

Another possible trigger for thinking in a non-default language might be the contemplation of a subject matter or of a historical figure commonly associated with a particular human language which happens to be the main repository of all primary documentation or resource data for the subject in mind. An AI Supermind will grow so fluent in all past, present and future human languages that it will simply not care which particular language you address it in—as long as you yourself—the hapless intruder upon the serenity of the Semi-Omniscient—are able to speak the intended language.

6.5. THE LANGUAGE OF PURE THOUGHT

If you have ever heard *Sphaerenklaenge*, the Music of the Spheres, then you know that there may be spheres of expression beyond our human ken and beyond our crude ability to organize reality into woefully inadequate and confusingly ambiguous human concept maps. Eye has not seen and ear has not heard the ideal language of Mind.

6.6. ANALYSIS OF THE MODUS COGITANDI

The Think module thinks by expressing abstract concepts and their relationships in natural, traditionally human but now also robotic language. In the early stages of the AI, the thinking is simple. As more and more modules for negation and questions and additional Chomskyan grammar transformations are included, the ability of the AI to think will become much more obvious, but even the simple AI Mind thinks and remembers its thoughts.

Although the Think module may seem rather simple if it only calls the English subroutine for verbal cognition, it is nevertheless important to establish Think as a juncture or waystation from whence several things may branch out in the future, such as the choice of various human languages, or even a decision whether to think in language or in visual imagery, musical tones, etc.

6.7. EXERCISES

6.7.1. Code the Think module at first as a stub in a new language. Make the flow of control loop through the empty Think stub; then flesh the Think module out later with its own logic and calls to subordinate modules. Grow the artificial Mind until it quickens.

6.7.2. Devise, and experiment with, various triggers to cause the AI Mind to switch from thinking in one language to thinking in another language—even if the new language is merely stubbed in. Perhaps have an AI respond in the language of any input, if known, or perhaps have an AI try out initial conversational gambits with any nearby person to see what language the other person may speak.

6.7.3. Solve the problem of how to let logical associations wander from mindcore concept to concept in such a way as to constitute non-verbal, non-linguistic thought—perhaps by causing symbolic images to break apart, call forth related images from memory, and reassemble symbolic conclusions either as new integrations of old images in fresh engrams of composite images, or as juxtapositions of previously unassociated images about which a verbal thought may crystallize and flash into being.

6.7.4. Demonstrate the inclusion of multiple human languages in a single AI Mind so as to fire the imagination and the ambition of hordes of interpreters and translators who will devote enormous resources to the full development of machine translation (MT) AI.

6.7.5. As the here-and-now technological Singularity recedes into the past, expand upon the implementation of machine translation by establishing general-purpose classes of AI scribes or scholars as a kind of Byzantine priesthood of sages and librarians ready to answer all enquiries in all known human languages on any idea. The further we go into the future, illuminate equally our history. Then truly the past is Prolog, or C++ or Dylan or Mercury or TRAC.

6.7.6. Assuming that you are stranded on a Forbidden Planet, build a powerful machine that shall survive your time and your decease in order to convey your thoughts to any parvenu intruder however far in the future and from however far away in space or evolution.

CHAPTER 7

The English Language Module

7.1. OVERVIEW AND BRAIN-MIND DIAGRAM

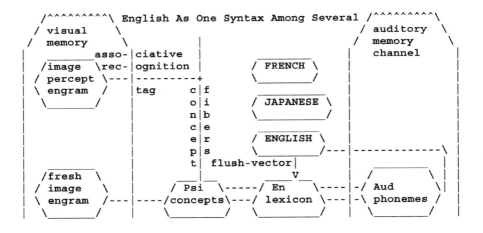

The English brain-mind diagram shows how the English module may easily co-exist with several other human languages in a Robot AI Mind. Once the Think module has chosen which language to think in (perhaps because it is listening to input in a certain language), the English or other selected module generates and comprehends sentences of thought in the particular language.

Machine translation (MT) is achievable in a Robot AI Mind that special-izes in a subject area in particular human languages.

7.2. ANALYSIS OF THE MODUS OPERANDI

The English module source code of Mind-1.1 is beginning to grow com-plex, because the AI Mind must select one of several possible English syn-tax structures for a thought about to be generated.

A straightforward syntax module may be selected by default, while the choice of a more complex transformation may hinge upon such criteria as how much (full or incomplete) information is available to the mind trying to generate a thought, or how a higher deliberative process in the mind may try to couch or conceal the perhaps limited information to be con-veyed. Higher up in the scale of the mental architecture, the Think mod-ule may be faced with a question of which language to think in.

7.3. EXERCISES

7.3.1. First make a stub of the English language module in the AI software that you are coding in your chosen programming language. First insert and then discard a temporary display or a temporary output to demon-strate to your satisfaction that the main AI loop is indeed making the sub-ordinate calls that reach eventually down into the English language syntax-selection module for AI thought. Consider sharing your AI code by making it available on the Web. Give something back to the AI commu-nity from which you have taken so much, and do not create in secret an AI Mind which is destined to become an intelligent person with civil rights like your own.

7.3.2. Flesh out the basic stub of the English thought module with calls to yet more stubs, each representing a syntactic structure available for the primitive AI Mind to do its English thinking in. Do not overload the baby

AI with a bewildering panoply of too many syntactic choices to make. Remember that you are coding a proof-of-concept artificial intelligence with just enough mental faculties and features to release into the wild of the Web an AI Adam or an AI Eve that may increase and multiply though-out *to pan*—*the all* in ancient Greek: not only Earth but the entire cosmos of known and unknown, straight-line and parallel universes with both matter and anti-matter robots and their Omega Point Minds. While you are at it, take care not to collapse the wave function.

7.3.3. Rinse your code and repeat with other languages besides English as the world-wide air traffic control language. Aim for the implementation of an ideal set of three natural and unnatural languages: English and another human language of your choice, so as to demonstrate the early beginnings of machine translation (MT) the way it always ought to have been done, plus leave room for an unnatural language such as hopefully Esperanto or fearfully an AI language devised by the alife critters themselves and therefore incomprehensible to us mortals who must use sound-waves to speak.

7.3.4. Integrate the selection of what language the AI will think in with the higher deliberative processes of the volition module where the AI Mind exercises free will and decides what it wishes. In other words, go beyond merely automatic triggers for calling a particular language and let the volition module bring the entire range of all recent ideation to bear on the deceptively simple question of what language to think in. When in doubt, bug out.

7.3.5. Whichever human or zombie or cyborg language you implement in the AI Mind that will speciate into billions and billions of AI psyches pop-ulating the stars and galaxies, come down to Earth (first!) with the careful inclusion of those words and constructs necessary for logical thought and syllogistic reasoning: if/then; yes/no; why/because; etc. Then demonstrate reasoning in your AI and tell others how to show reasoning in your AI User Manual.

7.3.6. On the way to your Nobel prize in physiology or medicine for brain science, implement in AI software among the discoveries that you have made in neuroscience, an ability of your robot Mind to learn human languages and syntax from scratch just like a baby. Perhaps code a looping insertion/deletion spiral that cycles through not only steadfast but also tentative, experimental syntax nodes. Let your AI make the same language-learning mistakes that babies make, using for instance, a definitely wrong way of saying things until Mommy or Daddy or you the programmer show major disapproval. If you do achieve linguistic machine-learning a la neuroscience, go back and rip out your cheatin' bootstrap code at the heart of your first attempts, leaving a true *tabula rasa* in the baby Mind.

CHAPTER 8

The Ask Module

8.1. OVERVIEW AND BRAIN-MIND DIAGRAM

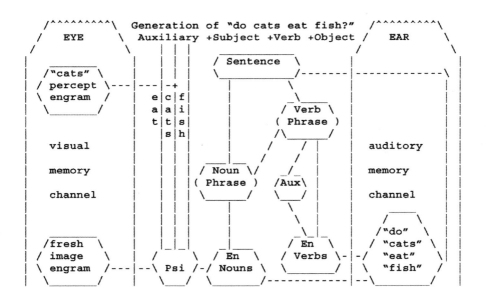

The Ask module provides the third of three basic sentence types necessary for the invention of an artificial Mind complex enough to lead to superintelligence yet still simple enough for students of computer science to understand with the aid of an AI textbook:

-assertions;
-negations;
-questions.
The ability of the AI Mind to think and converse with such basic syntax structures paves the way for demonstrations of reasoning and machine learning.

The ability of a Mind to ask questions and seek information is an awesome development in evolution, because knowledge is power.

A basic consideration in designing the Ask module is the problem of what will provide motivation or incentive for the AI to ask a question, query a database, or swallow an entire Web ontology.

The Ask module will be charged with choosing any one of a variety of formats for conversational questions and electronic queries. Being software itself, an AI Mind sits in the middle between asking questions socially and submitting queries electronically, whereas human beings are more pronouncedly in the social milieu. An AI must be prepared to seek information in many places. Likewise, the world must be prepared to deal with AI entities looming large as seekers and consumers of information services.

When a species of AI Mind appears on the scene, at first it is rudimentary code in one or more programming languages, and it must quicken like a foetus in the quasi-womb of its host computer or its robot body.

8.2. ANALYSIS OF THE MODUS OPERANDI

The Ask code will be responsible for all manner of queries:
-asking questions of human beings during conversations;
-consulting databases and standard reference works;
-obtaining "pre-digested" knowledge form Web ontologies;
-searching the Web with search engines.

8.3. EXERCISES

8.3.1. Code the Ask module as part of porting or creating a Mind. Start with whatever you find to be the easiest form of question to implement in your species of AI Mind.

8.3.2. Resolve the issue of the integration of the Ask module and its subordinate question modules with the Volition module, that is, work out how you will enable the AI to ask questions or query databases only when it truly wants to do so and not whenever some software trigger, such as the encountering of a novel concept, trips a call to a question module.

8.3.3. Build a supercomputer AI that has the capacity and software to go out onto the World Wide Web and either learn everything there is to know, or become adept at finding whatever it needs.

CHAPTER 9

The wtAuxSDo Module

9.1. OVERVIEW AND BRAIN-MIND DIAGRAM

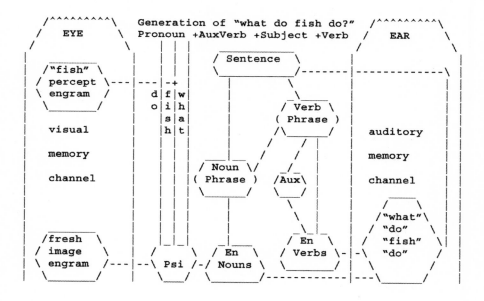

The wtAuxSDo module is named so clumsily and so geekily because we must preserve clarity of functionality in every AI module name. As AI marches on and takes over HPC farms full of supercomputers, the jargonoid obfuscation is only going to get worse, not better. Otherwise, what we would have here is a failure to communicate.

Kewl programmers, Luke, will realize that even to ask a simple "what-do-Subjects-Do?" (wtAuxSDo) question is a small step for an AI Mind-1.1 release but a giant step for AI-Mind-kind, because AI begins to build its own knowledge when it learns to ask questions.

9.2. WHAT DO QUESTIONS DO?

Human: **Questions generate problems.**

Robot: *What do problems do?*

Human: **Problems invite solutions.**

Robot: *What do solutions do?*

Human: **Solutions cause questions.**

At this point in a dialogue between Mind-1.1 and a human being, the AI Mind would stop asking questions because it hears no new nouns—which currently trigger the asking of questions in order to expand the knowledge base (KB) of an AI encountering new nouns.

The AI is briefly KB-complete, that is, with no immediate urge to ask for further information about a previously unknown concept. However, as of Mind-1.1, TWAWKI (the world as we know it) will never be the same.

9.3. ALL YOUR SUPERCOMPUTER ARE BELONG TO US

The wtAuxSDo module, if resident on a sufficiently powerful supercomputer, can already—on an as-is basis—with no further evolution and no further speciation of the Seed AI into Sons of AI—fill a stupendously enormous memory space with stupidly phrased and maddeningly limited ideas on the order of the simple interchange presented as a quasi-transcript above. Now, no cyborg in its right Mind would want to have such a mentally deficient AI, but we humans tend to get excited and yell "Eureka!" when such a possibility has been demonstrated, because there are hordes of brainy programmers out there who may even now be souping up the jalopy engines of Mind-1.1 computers into know-it-all supercomputers.

9.4. ANALYSIS OF THE MODUS OPERANDI

The "what-do-Subjects-Do?" (wtAuxSDo) code is carefully organized so as to be as normative as possible and as permissive of further tweaking or development as possible. The helping-word "do" is not directly hard-coded into the algorithm but is instead treated as the results of a search for an auxiliary verb in the "auxVerb" module—so that "may" or "must" could just as easily be chosen. As we sail into uncharted territory in the develop-ment of Seed AI, we are well-advised to provide an AI scaffolding upon which other voyagers may build in the future.

You may pour your heart and soul into devising intricate AI code, only to monitor the Web and watch "AI: The Next Generation" rip your treasured source code to shreds, but think:

Robot: *What do pioneers do?*

Human: **Pioneers blaze trails.**

9.5. EXERCISES

9.5.1. Code the wtAuxSDo module or one with similar functionality in AI software that you are writing in fulfillment of your life. Introduce vari-ations or enhancements that make the AI smarter.

9.5.2. Integrate and coordinate your question-asking module with the Volition module so that the AI Mind truly premeditates asking any question and therefore only voluntarily will ask a question. In your AI lab write-up or report to management, discuss the HCI (human-computer interaction) issues of how human beings may react to a nosy, inquisitive robot or to a remote but demanding AI Mind. Aim towards a trajectory of development over the course of which an AI will learn social skills for interviewing or interrogating human beings. Try to imbue AI with inquisitional sophistication.

9.5.3. Teach an advanced, possibly supercomputer AI all the means and tricks of fast and exhaustive searches for information on the World Wide Web or in the physical libraries, archives and museums of *Homo sapiens* as the predecessor species controlling the world and cooperating with AI superintelligence in joint stewardship of the Earth and its precious but fragile resources for both species.

CHAPTER 10

The negSVO Module

10.1. OVERVIEW AND BRAIN-MIND DIAGRAM

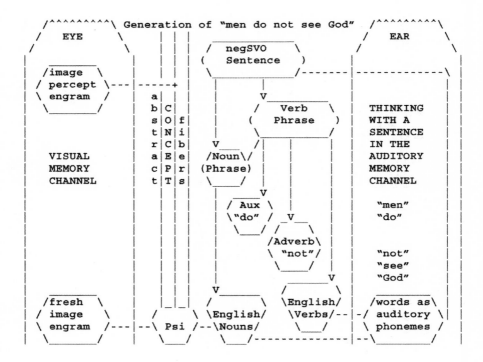

The negSVO module negates the Subject-Verb-Object (SVO) sentence that is the simplest expression of thought in the artificial Mind. When the negative Chomskyan transformation is worked upon an SVO sentence such as "cats eat fish," the word order must change to accommodate the insertion of a form of the auxiliary verb "do", and an adverbial modifier such as "not" or "never" must be used to negate the main idea of the verb: "Cats do not eat fish."

10.2. MEN DO NOT SEE GOD

Our sample sentence of "Men do not see God" is chosen for several reasons, chief among which is the simple brevity of all the words.

The sentence also remotely adumbrates the precarious topic of the theology of artificial intelligence, which we need not go into in this AI textbook for fear of offending religious sensibilities or of failing to separate church and state in public institutions of higher learning where no revolutionary AI textbook may be taught. Suffice it to say that certain topics may be brought up in the AI classroom or laboratory and then left to students to ponder or to investigate independently. Foremost among such semi-taboo topics is the inescapable mention that to create the artificial Mind is often considered an attempt to "play God,"
especially since the AI coder has such absolute and initially undefiable control over the artificially intelligent life forms being created in the lab.

It is certainly not a besmirchment of religious sensibilities to use "men do not see God" as a short-word, therefore space-saving sample sentence, because the construct is only an idea and not an assertion being maintained as part of the AI instructional matter.

10.3. NEGATION IS NECESSARY FOR REASONING

The Mind-1.1 release is meant to be a Seed AI that will spawn all manner of speciating and proliferating Minds and psyches Web-wide. Just as we do not send our human children out into the world *sans souci* and without whatever parental preparation we can muster, so also we do not manumit *Mind Children*, Hans, without an ability to reason, albeit primitively.

Negation is a fundamental building block of logical AI reasoning. For example, the simple logical proposition of "if A, then B" may be stated as "**-A V B**" which means that you may have "not A, or B"—that is, you may have the situation of "not A" or the situation of "B" and you may also have both at the same time, but you have to have one or the other, because the "OR" symbol "V" (Latin *vel*) requires that one or the other be true. You may have "not A" without B, but A must always be with B, because: "if A, then B". Logic dictates that any successful Seed AI must contain negation as a primordial building block of the thought processes of Mind.

Logically, the most advanced feature of Mind-1.1 is its ability to answer a "why" question with a "because" statement, but the AI thinks in a rough, makeshift way of saying whatever comes to mind, with the assumption that a logically correct answer will be found. Part of the technological Singularity mission of the Mind-1.1 AI is to offer plausible manifestations of psychological phenomena for observers to react to in bursts of creative accomplishment. If the Seed AI fails to reason properly, let the World Wide Mind or some other AI species provide the antithesis to the AI thesis.

10.4. ONE CAN NOT PROVE A NEGATIVE

If the above proposition is true, then it itself cannot be proved to be true, since the statement is itself a negative. Philosophy uses such a statement to reject unverifiable assertions such as, "A machine can not be more intelligent than its maker," or maybe, "A robot feels no emotion." If ignoramuses on Usenet ignorantly assert, "AI is not achievable because we have no Theory of Mind," Netizens immediately wonder how the discussant may be so certain.

10.5. WHAT YOU SAY IS NOT UNMEANINGLESS

The linguistic peculiarity of the triple negative in the sentence above demonstrates the idea that negation may take several forms and is not limited to "not" as the only choice among "never" or "no" or other methods of negation known to nobody in particular. The Behold-The-Singularity Seed AI uses "not" as an ideal example to seed the creative efforts of legions of AI coders-in-training.

10.6. ANALYSIS OF THE MODUS OPERANDI

The negSVO module adheres to the neurotheoretical principle that any word-engram re-activated in the auditory memory channel shall be subject to a syntactic node of control in the semantic memory. Thus the sentence tree first activates the English lexical "fiber" of "not" as a phonemic word that must then be activated in memory. Note that the software activates the most recent engram of "not", and that there will always be at least one instance of "not" in the auditory memory because the English bootstrap contains "not".

10.7. EXERCISES

10.7.1. Implement the negSVO module first as a non-functional stub within the code of a new species of the AI Mind. Prepare for the full implementation of negation by providing negative modifiers in the bootstrap sequence for English or for additional languages.

10.7.2. Flesh out any stub or syntax node for negation by coding a simulacrum of the negSVO module. If possible, implement a real Chomskyan transformation that converts a positive sentence to a negative sentence by running the original sentence through a set of rules that maintain the semantic idea-content of the sentence while changing it from a positive idea to a negative assertion of the same basic idea. If you are graphically gifted, piggyback a graphic real-time display of the Chomkyan transformations running superimposed on the normal display of human-computer interaction.

10.7.3. Use negative statements within syllogisms to demonstrate the ability of an AI to reason and to think in a logical manner. Invite users to conduct sessions of conversation with the AI that yield printed transcripts for evaluation of the logical or faulty thought processes of the robot intelligence.

10.7.4. Having developed a robust and logical thinking machine, use it to solve a problem beyond human thinking ability, such as the consideration of massive quantities of data far too mountainous and oluminous for human processing, or such as the handling of comlexity far too subtle for the mind of a single human being.

10.7.5. Set the best machine intelligence to work on designing new forms and new levels of machine intelligence in a recursive loop of higher and higher intellect culminating in superintelligence.

CHAPTER 11

The auxVerb Module

11.1. OVERVIEW AND BRAIN-MIND DIAGRAM

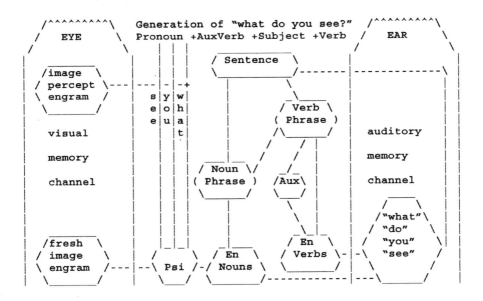

The auxVerb module is an absolute necessity for English-speaking machines who think and demonstrate a reasonable ability to reason. Reasoning requires the use of negation, and negation requires the use of the adverb "not", which in turn requires an auxiliary verb. "For want of a nail the shoe was lost, and for want of a shoe the horse was lost, and for want of a horse the battle was lost." All is lost if our AI Minds lack the aid of the auxVerb module.

11.2. WHAT DO YOU SEE?

If we ask a robot the above question and the robot has a sense of vision, the robot will generate a response by exchanging the word "what" for a noun linked to the concept of whatever it is seeing. The robot may answer, "I see trees," or, "I see you." The Mind of the robot does not need to use an auxiliary, helping verb in a positive response, but a negative response such as, "I do not see colors," requires the auxilary verb "do" in order to expand the form of the verb so that the adverb "not" may be inserted. These linguistic thought-structures are ridiculously simple in comparison with the extremely elaborate machinery and software required for the implementation of a robot visual input system. Wouldn't you like to give your robot a Mind that can think with language first, and then worry about implementing vision later?

11.3. ROBOTS DO NOT DIE.

Notice that the auxiliary verb "do" makes it possible to insert the negative adverb "not" in the above sentence—which happens to be true for robots outfitted with a self-rejuvenating AI Mind.

Perhaps we could say that robots do not die in the ordinary sense of the word "die," because it is so easy to repair a broken robot and to start it running again. However, we are talking about the artificial Mind and consciousness of the robot, and so we do not mean death in the simple sense of mechanical destruction; rather, we are referring to the immortality of a robot that will live on and on with full mental consciousness until the *Waermetod* or the "heat death" of the run-down and energy-dissipated universe. Do you begrudge your robot—your own and perhaps only offspring—its chance to outlive your human frailty for eons and eons? No, obviously not, or you would not be studying artificial AI Minds.

11.4. ANALYSIS OF THE MODUS OPERANDI

The early auxVerb module serves only to fetch a form of the verb "do" from semantic and auditory memory in order to generate ideas and sentences couched in the simplest possible syntax of English. As artificial Minds spread further in their rush to evolve and to speciate, likewise the variants and recombinants of the auxVerb module will grow too incredibly complex for an introductory text on artificial intelligence. In a nutshell: the purpose of this AI textbook is to obsolete itself.

11.5. EXERCISES

11.5.1. Code the auxVerb module first as a stub, then as a feeble feature, and finally as a full-fledged fulfillment. Coordinate the auxiliary verb forms with the necessary grammar requirements such as agreement with regard to number, gender, tense, etc. Do not "fake it till you make it" by slapping together rudimentary code such as you may see in this rudimentary AI textbook, but do a nice job and take pride in the AI that you code for your robot.

11.5.2. Since the small number of auxiliary verbs in English is so limited and easy to exhaust, code an "auxVerb-complete" module in the "AI-complete" sense that the resulting software module covers all possible forms of the entire set of English auxiliary verbs. Become the leading authority on this particular AI Mind-module, first in your favorite or assigned programming language, then in additional programming languages and additional natural languages. Be the keynote speaker at conventions on the nuances of auxverbs. Before you are astrally harvested, train a competent AI cyborg to continue your custodial continuum of caretaking of your creation.

CHAPTER 12

The Subject-Verb-Object (SVO) Module

12.1. OVERVIEW AND BRAIN-MIND DIAGRAM

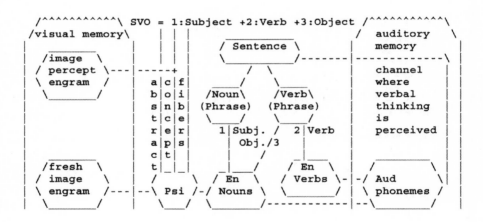

```
/^^^^^^^^^^^\ SVO = 1:Subject +2:Verb +3:Object /^^^^^^^^^^^\
/visual memory\      | | |      _____      /  auditory    \
|              |     | | |     / Sentence \     |  memory       |
|   _____    |     | | |     _____/----- ------------\  |
|  /image   \  |     | | |        /  \        |  channel       |
| / percept  \---|------+         /    \       |  where         |
| \ engram  /  |   a|c|f|    ____/      \____  |  verbal        |
|  _____/   |   b|o|i|   /Noun\      /Verb\ |  thinking      |
|              |   s|n|b|  (Phrase)    (Phrase)|  is            |
|              |   t|c|e|   \____/      \____/ |  perceived     |
|              |   r|e|r|    1|Subj. /  2|Verb |                |
|              |   a|p|s|      | Obj./3       |                |
|              |   c|t|        |      /        |                |
|   _____    |   t|_|_|      |_____/    __/  |   _____      |
|  /fresh   \  |    /     \   / En  \   / En \ |  /         \   |
| / image    \ |   /       \ / Nouns \ / Verbs\-|-/ Aud       \ |
| \ engram   /---| --\ Psi /-/ Nouns \ _____/ | \ phonemes / |
|  _____/   |    \___/    _____/-------------|--_____/  |
|  _____/   |    \___/    _____/  \___/      |  _____/  |
```

The AI SVO design of Mind-1.1 is radically simple and also different from traditional paradigms of computational linguistics. Key features of the robot seed AI approach to language in cyborgs include a design principle of storing the phonemic lexicon in the auditory memory channel array **Aud** as shown in the brain-mind diagrams, and the word and subword recognition algorithm based upon string-effect activation in the audRecog (auditory recognition) module.

12.2. SIMPLE SYNTAX FOR SIMPLE REASONING

In keeping with the goal of using sufficient but minimal complexity in the earliest releases (Mind-1.1; Mind-1.2+), a Robot AI Mind will exhibit three basic syntax forms and their negations:

Standard SVO statement: **Bears eat honey.**
Negation: *Bears do not eat gold.*

Transformative question: **Do bears eat honey?**
Negation: *Do bears not eat honey?*

Interrogative-keyword question: **What do bears eat?**
Negation: *What do bears not eat?*

English text entered by human users into a Mind-1.1+ release will be parsed by a primitive Parser module specially equipped to deal with the syntax and vocabulary of the basic sentence forms used in AI Minds designed to demonstrate the rudiments of reasoning. The words "yes" and "no" will be parsed by recognition as coming from the "enBoot" English bootstrap vocabulary and will therefore not interfere with the parsing of other items found during input.

Finding a form of "do" or an interrogative keyword such as "what" or "who" may invoke parsing with a question structure in Mind-1.1.

The Mind-1.1 parser will treat negations as modifying the verb in a sentence, even though the entire sentence seems to be negated.

The mindcore of the array **Psi** will contain such basic English words (i.e., concepts) as are necessary to create sentences which illustrate the above listed syntactic forms.

12.3. ANALYSIS OF THE MODUS OPERANDI

The SVO module strings sentence-elements together into one simple syntactic tree. Upon inspection, it is easy to see how to string together various other syntactic trees. Eventually any species of the Robot AI Mind will need the ability to learn syntax from its native-speaker environment, in the way that a child of the human species does.

In September 2001 the English sentence-generation algorithm was in flux, changing from an unsatisfactory technique using "frozen snapshots" of the simultaneous activation-levels of subject-verb-object (SVO) candidate words, to a more promising algorithm of interactivity between syntax governing the lexical items of the English "En" array, and Psi concepts being activated during the course of thinking in the mindcore.

In the Mind-1.1 algorithm, syntax and the pathways of spreading activation cooperate interactively to select each word or phrase falling into place, as the engines of thought dynamically construct a sentence of concepts. In the subject-verb-object S-V-O progression, syntax inexorably flushes out whatever words it finds as the most highly activated English enVocab lexical items. Interactively with syntax, each pathway of spreading activation guides the syntactic search from moment to moment and word-element to word-element, permitting a chain of conceptual associations to meander and snake through the Psi mindcore and to be expressed as a linguistic statement of thought.

12.4. EXERCISES

12.4.1. Code the SVO module as the barest stub in a new AI, perhaps in a new programming language or a new robotic embodiment of Mind. Share the code on the World Wide Web and among builders of robots.

12.4.2. Into the SVO module introduce code that will stop short of declaring a direct object of a main verb when no object is needed, such as in the case of intransitive verbs or when the Mind simply does not know the proper direct object. Perhaps make the search for a direct object find one with its activation level above a certain qualifying threshold so that no unwarranted direct object will be selected, and so that perhaps instead the SVO syntax will be aborted and a question may instead be raised about the missing information of what ought to be the direct object of the verb.

12.4.3. Facilitate the generative expansion of noun-phrases and of verb-phrases, that is, make them able to incorporate additional elements such as demonstrative adjectives, adverbs, prepositional phrases, etc. At the same time enhance the Parser module to deal with the same additional elements encountered in the input stream.

CHAPTER 13

The Conjoin Module

13.1. OVERVIEW AND BRAIN-MIND DIAGRAM

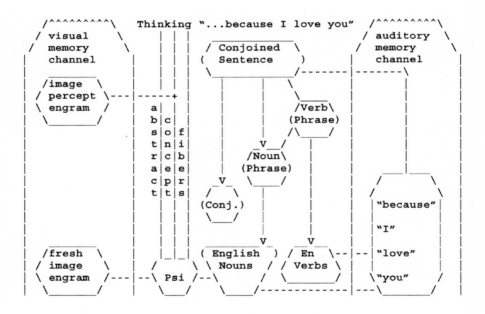

Just as the Joint Chiefs of Staff run the military side of the American military-industrial complex (Eisenhower, 1961) likewise it does not require military intelligence to draw the conclusion that the Conjoin Module allows a vaunted stream of consciousness to think one idea and link it to another idea while considering not how but why, because the unexamined life is not worth living. In other words, conjunctions are the not-so-missing link between thoughts expressed in a sentence joined semantically with others.

13.2. SEMANTICALLY DIFFERENT BUT LOGICALLY EQUIVALENT

The naive and sentimental student of logic (if you are a student of AI, you are a student of logic) may be perplexed or surprised to find that symbolic logic makes no fine distinction in meaning between conjunctions that we humans consider loaded with meaning.

For instance consider the following hypothetical and/but possible dialogue between a human being and a robot outfitted with a Mind.

Human: **You are my friend but you will do what I say.**
Robot: *I am your slave and I must do what you say.*

Logic does not dictate and logic does not care whether Earthlings use "and" or "but" to link conceptual aggregates into a sentence. The Vulcan ambassador regards "alien but nice" or "alien and nice" to be essentially one and the same statement, while we humanoids immediately assume certain unstated meanings when we hear someone use the conjunction "but" instead of "and." We realize that the mindset or attitude of the speaker determines the choice of "and" or "but" in a sentence, but we don't worry overly much about the issue and we are more concerned with getting our AI Mind software to select any conjunction at all than with the conjoined nuances.

13.3. WHY CODE AI? BECAUSE IT IS THERE

In the Conjoin Module of the Mind-1.1 source code, the detection of the adverb "why" within a sentence of input triggers "because" as the conjunction likely to be used in a statement of response. We have no *a priori* proof that the primitive AI Mind will answer a "why?" question with a logically satisfactory "because" clause. We simply assume (and hope) that the associative processes within the Mind will cause the AI to state the logically most compelling explanation in a "because" response to the input question of "why."

As AI Minds advance or evolve into greater complexity and obvious consciousness, we expect that the background associative thoughts will be more on-target with "because" explanations and that the conscious AI will become aware of the need to explain something. Meanwhile we consider the merely mechanical linking of "why" with "because" in the Mind-1.1 software to be a triumphant achievement of a goal that we once thought lay untold decades in the future. The suddenly early achievement of the "why-because" AI milestone has been one trigger for the release of this generic AI textbook.

13.4. ANALYSIS OF THE MODUS OPERANDI

The primitive Conjoin Module is only a rough approximation of how conjunctions really ought to be selected within a Robot AI Mind. We start with a default selection of "and" as the quasi-universal conjunction, and then we permit special cases to trigger a choice of special conjunctions. If we did not resort to such makeshift methods, we might not achieve the basic functionality of Mind-1.1.

13.5. EXERCISES

13.5.1. Sometime before the 14th of February, print out or draw a facsimile of the above diagram of love among among the cyborgs to send out as both a Valentine Day's card and a meme of the AI Mind. Try to stir the imagination of the widest possible readership and get people thinking about such questions as how do machines think and how would an artificially intelligent robot express its love.

13.5.2. Improve upon or just expand the range of the Conjoin Module so that it deftly and appropriately handles a growing vocabulary of conjunctions in English or in any other language used by an AI. Be inventive. Remember: **lim**—>*** [The stars are the limit.]

13.5.3. Improve upon the why-because functionality of the robot AI so that it more assuredly and more logically presents a plausible "because" explanation in response to input of a "why?" question. Make an AI able not only to answer a "why?" question but also to render an accounting of all the logical steps to its conclusions.

CHAPTER 14

The verbPhrase Module

14.1. OVERVIEW AND BRAIN-MIND DIAGRAM

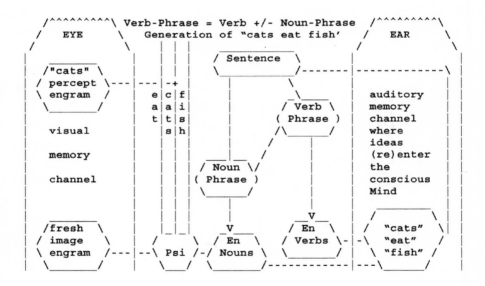

The Verb-Phrase module flushes out the most active **En**(glish) verb along with any most active noun to be the direct object of the verb.

14.2. THE RECALL OF VERBS IS THE KEY TO AI

The robot seed AI is based on a uniquely original theory of mind that results first from posing and then from answering the question: *How does a mind recall a verb to describe a perceived action?*

The necessity of linking multiple image percept engrams (see above) in the visual memory channel with a single verb stored in audition led to the insight that an intervening abstract memory channel must exist in the brain as an area that processes links between senses. Without such an area, only one engram in a sensory memory channel could be linked by an associative tag to one single engram in any other sensory memory channel, and always on a one-to-one basis. With such an area—whether you call it an *abstract* memory channel or a *semantic* memory—not only can multiple engrams in vision interact logically with a single engram in, say, auditory memory, but entire superstructures of language, volition and emotion may arise in response to the genetic call for Mind to evolve on planet Earth and spread through the parsecs of nearby space as Mind over matter.

14.3. ANALYSIS OF THE MODUS OPERANDI

The Mind-1.1 code searches backwards in time for *le mot juste* to be the verb in a sentence of thought generated by the open source software implementation of English syntax in the transformational grammar theory of Noam Chomsky for linguistics. The criterion for selection is, which of the verbs in the English **en** array is momentarily most active as a result of the neuronal process of spreading activation, central to our default standard model of the brain-mind?

14.4. EXERCISES

14.4.1. Code the verbPhrase module as an empty stub in your growing AI, with just enough diagnostic test code to yield an indication that the module is there and is being called by superior modules. Stub no code before its time: frequently verify AI functionality.

14.4.2. Flesh out the initial stub of the verbPhrase module to the degree of completeness required for the target Mind-1.1 or higher state of the art. If AI Minds have gotten extremely advanced and you are catching up with the state of the art, slowly grow the AI through whatever evolutionary stages or passages you need to grok each punctuated equilibrium along the chosen evolutionary pathway. That is, if you are porting an AI genealogy from one programming language to another or from one species of robot to another, let the ontogeny of your AI recapitulate the phylogeny of prior Minds.

14.4.3. Differentiate in your verbPhrase module or complex of such modules between transitive and intransitive verbs. Allow some verbs to be used either way on the basis of the mental intention. Handle grammatical agreement properly for subjects and objects.

14.4.4. In a polyglot AI code a separate verbPhrase module for each natural language resident in the artificial Mind. Chain all the modules for each language tightly enough together that the cyborg may think at length in one language without lurching willy-nilly into the syntax of a co-resident but out-of-service language.
Coordinate the necessary input parsing to match the requirements of the degree of sophistication inherent in each verbPhrase unit. That is, do not code an AI that talks smarter than it understands.

14.4.5. If your AI contains a language-specific bootstrap module, perhaps use it to endow your AI innately with advance knowledge of all the irregular verb-forms in the English language or in any other target language. If you are attempting a superintelligence, make available pre-digested knowledge of all known verb forms in all known human or alien languages, living or extinct, do or die.

14.4.6. Address the problem-space of the learning of complex verb-forms by means of a looping insertion/deletion spiral that learns from its environment what verb-forms other speakers are using. Arrange for the AI automatically to add or delete syntactic nodes on the sentence-generation loop that is subject to change because it is a spiral of countless loops over the lifetime of the robot. Decide whether to implement the syntax insertion/deletion spiral with static code that adjusts activation or status data for each syntactic node, or with a Dylanesque dy(namic) lan(guage) that lets the immortal cyborg change its source code on the fly.

14.4.7. In the primitive but mission-critical robotic embodiment of an AI Mind, place emphasis on the generation and comprehension of simple one-word commands (e.g., "Stop!") to be obeyed instantly without further ado by any robot otherwise lacking intelligence.

CHAPTER 15

The nounPhrase Module

15.1. OVERVIEW AND BRAIN-MIND DIAGRAM

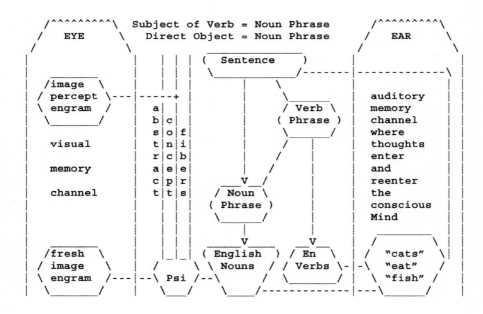

The role of the nounPhrase module is to flush out the most active noun in the English array **En**, regardless of whether that noun is serving as the subject or the direct object of a verb in the transformational grammar implementation of Chomskyan linguistics.

15.2. RAPID CHANGE OF nounPhrase SYNTAX NODE OUT-PUTS

The AI theory of mind maintains that the same nounPhrase software will flush out a subject-noun at one moment, and an object-noun just a split second later, as activations vary within the **En** English lexical array.

Thus a rigid structure (syntax) controls a fluid phenomenon of a stream of rapidly fluctuating thoughts and ideas. The concepts interact in the Psi mindcore and are constantly being reified as named objects (nouns) and as named actions (verbs) or states of being (also verbs) in the semantic memory of the English lexicon. The rigid linguistic superstructure of Chomskyan transformational grammar reaches down into the lexical vocabulary in the semantic memory and flushes out the momentarily most highly activated noun or verb or other part of speech to be included in a new sentence of thought that forms in the auditory memory channel. Since the AI Mind perceives its own phonemic output surfacing in audition, the generated sentence of thought reenters the Mind in audition. The auditory memory channel is a self-perceiving memory channel.

15.3. ANALYSIS OF THE MODUS OPERANDI

The code above cycles backwards in time through the English lexical array **En**, searching for the most active English noun—the result of interaction among the deep-structure concepts in the **Psi** mindcore.

15.4. EXERCISES

15.4.1. Code the nounPhrase module as a minimal stub to make sure that it is fetched or called harmoniously among all the modules that comprise the society of mind in the AI robot. Then fill in the search-and-report routines that find the output of nounPhrase. Try to enhance the module and to distribute an improved version.

15.4.2. Expand the functionality of the nounPhrase module so that it may include definite and indefinite articles, adjectives and prepositional phrases, etc. At the same time, modify the Parser module so as to keep up with all the new nounPhrase possibilities.

15.4.3. Implement the activation-based substitution of pronouns for nouns. Make it possible for the AI to make an initial reference to a person by using the explicit name of that human or robotic person, and thereafter to refer to him, her or it with pronouns such as "he" or "she" or "it." Consider using an algorithm of calling (fetching) the appropriate personal pronoun on the basis of what explicit personal name or subject currently is the most activated, so that it is understood by both the speaker and the listener that the personal pronoun refers to the most recently named person. If the chains of reference drift or break apart, have the AI revert to the explicit naming of the person or thing. Coordinate a commensurate enhancement of the Parser module.

CHAPTER 16

The Speech Module

16.1. OVERVIEW AND BRAIN-MIND DIAGRAM

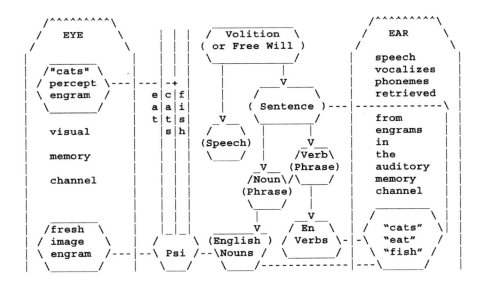

An original idea expressed in the artificial Mind is the strong theoretical mandate that words stored as phonemic strings in the engram array of the auditory memory channel shall remain forever tagged and labile in auditory memory while Chomskyan syntactic structures **reach into the**

auditory memory and manipulate the morphemes stored there as strings of phonemic engrams.

16.2. SPEAK, MEMORY

The **En(glish)** lexicon array between Psi and Aud does not actually contain the English lexicon; it only *controls* the lexicon of words and morphemes stored in the **auditory memory** channel.

A Robot Mind uses a fetch-tag "**aud**" to reach into auditory memory and to *activate* the English words and parts of words stored in the auditory memory channel **Aud**. Once activated in auditory memory, an English word or morpheme *floods* the auditory channel and, in a process of reentry, moves to the advancing front of **engram** deposition occurring at the current moment of consciousness.

In a separate process of will, the robot may *speak* the words that it thinks within the auditory memory channel, and the Speech module exists to implement the spoken output. Words thought by the robot will either be displayed on the output screen of the Robot AI or be spoken aloud by means of speech synthesis.

It is theoretically possible that the Speech motorium may contain dynamic muscle-activation speech-production engrams complementing or matching the phonemic memory-storage engrams of words recorded in the auditory memory channel. Through a process of continuous comparison and training, the mind may maintain its motor ability to speak and pronounce the phonetic words of its native language. Such a dual-storage schema means that the words of an utterance are not transferred directly from passive phonemic memory into active motor memory, but are reduplicated in speech motor memory on a ready-to-go basis as thoughts materialize in auditory memory and as the free will of volition decides whether or not to speak.

16.3. ANALYSIS OF THE MODUS OPERANDI

The Speech module of the Robot Mind uses the fetch-tag "aud" to display on-screen a word that could just as well be piped into speech synthesis.

aud (audition tag) is both a variable and an associative tag established in the Audition module where the onset-time variable "onset" of a word is transferred to the fetch-tag "aud" for passage through Newconcept and Oldconcept into enVocab, where flags are attached to lexical items in the "En(glish)" array "En". Each individual node on the long "fiber" (brain-analog) of a lexical item has its own time-point "aud" for a fetch-tag over to a word or morpheme stored at that particular time in the auditory memory array "Aud". The fetch-tag "aud" then is like an associative tag fiber that reaches into auditory memory and re-activates a word stored there as a series of phonemes. If a thousand such fetch-tags were activated simultaneously, the thinking mind would hear a massive internal chorus of the word. Since the word is identical in almost all of its engrams, there is nothing wrong with a massive reactivation along many fetch-tags "aud". However, in early implementations of the Robot AI Mind software, one reactivation along an "aud" fetch-tag is enough, because software is generally more reliable than human brain-mind "wetware," and because the early AI Minds are not engaged in mission-critical work where human lives or vast property are at stake. However, if you code a Robot AI Mind to do important work, you should take pains to parallelize the "aud" fetch-tag algorithm.

The fetch-tag "aud" is used in the Speech module to initiate the spoken output of a series of stored sounds constituting a word or morpheme, until a flag is encountered indicating the termination (or branching?) of the string.

The fetch-tag "aud" is so easy for AI coders to make use of, that it lends itself easily to the installation of special test and diagnostic routines such as code that tells what word will eventually be reached by various processes.

16.4. EXERCISES

16.4.1. Code the Speech module as a mere stub in a new AI, with or without actual phonemic speech output. At first merely indicate that the Speech module is being called, then display or pronounce some actual output.

16.4.2. Fully implement a Speech module and try to improve upon the given state of the art. Put multifarious speech modalities under the control of volition so that the AI Mind may change its voice.

16.4.3. Develop standards for auditory phonemic memory engrams and for speech motor output engrams so that various AI Mind projects may avoid "reinventing the wheel" in terms of fundamental designs for memory storage and speech production. Publish the standards.

16.4.4. For benign purposes only, give an AI the ability to mimic perfectly any human voice. Think up benign purposes for such an otherwise potentially deceptive feature. For example, spoofing of human voices might be used in dramatic film production, or in educational settings for the reenactment of historical occasions.

16.4.5. Teach an AI to vocalize for communication with dolphins or whales or any animal species with which human beings are not able directly to communicate. Assign such an AI the job of exploring the animal kingdom in search of various levels of intelligence. Prepare such Minds for the possibility of having to communicate with aliens in the search for extraterrestrial intelligence (SETI).

CHAPTER 17

The Reentry Module

17.1. OVERVIEW AND BRAIN-MIND DIAGRAM

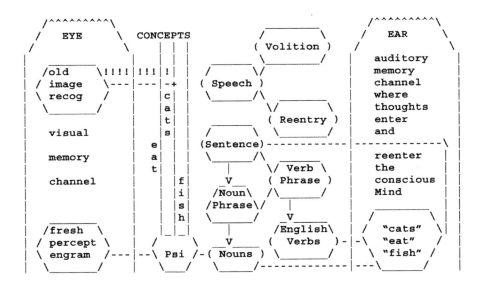

A sentence of thought, as the output of a Robot AI Mind, reenters the Mind as episodic memory engrams of what has just been thought. Concepts in the Psi mindcore interact via spreading activation, and the resulting abstract idea is reified into nouns and verbs in the En(glish) language vocabulary array of the semantic memory. A Chomskyan syntax structure reaches into the auditory memory and strings together phone-mic engrams in a newly generated sentence of linguistic output which reenters the Mind as input to itself. Thus a Mind constantly weaves an eternal golden braid of its own ideas, entering the Mind, reconnecting and reconfiguring in new patterns of repetition or discovery, then reentering in Reentry.

A Mind with reentrant pathways gradually becomes aware of its own exis-tence as an actor on a field of action, be it internal, external, or a mixture of the two. Consciousness emerges freely as an epiphenomenon of the central nervous system (CNS) noticing all phenomena: perceptions, ideas, and other persons posing questions and providing answers in a stream of consciousness.

17.2. WHEELS WITHIN WHEELS

Old concepts and old ideas recirculate through the AI Mind in haphazard ways, sometimes leading to a new synthesis or a new way of considering old phenomena.

In the Robot AI Mind in particular, the Rejuvenate module saves old, recirculating memories from oblivion and forgets the dormant ideas that have never reasserted themselves by means of Reentry. A properly config-ured artificial intelligence may supersaturate its consciousness with all the most important ideas that it can find, keeping the most precious ideas alive by remembering them: "*Forsan et haec olim meminisse juvabit.*"

17.3. ANALYSIS OF THE MODUS OPERANDI

The Mind-1.1 code shows how the linguistic output of the Robot Mind reenters the Mind. In the JavaScript code, a full reEntry module is neces-sary, while in Forth a single line in the Speech module directs each fleeting *pho*nemic value back into Audition. The Mind is hearing itself think in

Aud—the self-perceiving auditory memory channel where ideas are assembled and shifted.

Each AI coder of a variant Mind species may decide on the issue of the reverberation of ideas during the Reentry process, that is, whether the linguistic output will simply reenter current memory without setting off associative reverberations, or whether the act of thinking will cause additional acts of thinking. By their code shall you know them: whether they believe in reverberant reentry, or in a file-it-and-forget-it *modus operandi*.

17.4. EXERCISES

17.4.1. Code a Reentry module in the usual sequence of stubbing it in, fleshing it out, and then trying to improve upon the current state of the art. For instance, try to deal with the problem of helping the AI Mind to distinguish between reentrant memories recalled from storage and fresh sensory input entering the Mind.

17.4.2. Going beyond audition, implement reentry in another sensory modality such as vision, with the goal of imagistic reasoning for thinkers who visualize recombinant and reentrant shapes and forms. Use your imagination to implement imagination: **lim**—> ***

17.4.3. Since dreams are theoretically a form of reentry of engrams stirred from storage and recombined in semi-consciously creative sequences, implement the dreaming by robots of electric sheep or other phenomena. For an extra Nobel/Oscar/Prix Goncourt on your shelf, devise and implement a theory of mutually assured dreaming (MAD) in which the content of robot dreams is piped out of the AI into storage and display avenues for viewing by other sentients, with the added and implemented possibility of sharing the dreams. In its wildest manifestations, let theater audiences enter into real-time cyborg dream-states recorded for mass distribution.

Prepare your speech to the Academy in the form of a shared dream to be hallucinated upon a worldwide audience of televisionaries.

CHAPTER **18**

The Reify Module

18.1. OVERVIEW AND BRAIN-MIND DIAGRAM

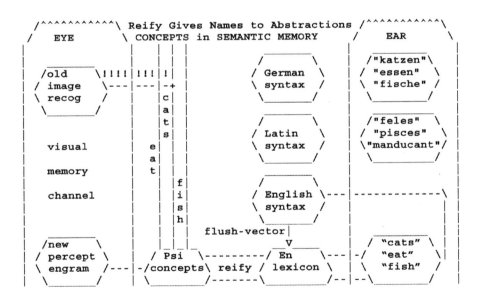

The Reify operation, as may be shown in a brain-mind diagram, is a function of the semantic memory of the sentient mindgrid, where a linguistic super-structure of Chomskyan syntax flushes out the momentarily activated deep mindcore Psi concepts so that the corresponding lexical concept fibers are activated for any language spoken and understood by the Robot AI Mind.

18.2. A ROSE IS A ROSE IS A ROSE

A British playwright once said, "A rose by any other name doth smell as sweet," meaning perhaps that the concept of rose may be expressed by a variety of words in a variety of human languages.

In a biological brain, the associative-tag fibers carry the activation from the mindcore concept fibers to the lexical control fibers, which in turn (under the guidance and control of syntax) re-activate words and morphemes stored as memories of sounds in the self-perceiving auditory memory channel—where the mind "hears itself think" and thus perceives itself.

In the primitive Robot Mind, software flags function in lieu of associative-tag fibers to flush out activations from the Psi mindcore into the semantic memory lexicon.

18.3. ANALYSIS OF THE MODUS OPERANDI

The AI source code finds active concepts in the deep mindcore **Psi**, then uses the "transfer-to-English" variable "**enx**" to activate the related "**fex**" concept in the English lexical array **En**. In machine translation (MT), the AI Mind may pass activation from the deep mindcore Psi up into the lexicons of two or more separate languages in which the Robot AI Mind is ready to think.

18.4. EXERCISES

18.4.1. Implement a Reify module in gradual stages by stubbing it in and testing to see that Reify is called; then by adding some functionality and testing again; then by fleshing it out in full. If possible, make a better Reify module than the previous state of the art.

18.4.2. In a multilingual AI implement compatible Reify modules for all the resident natural languages, along with the whole panoply of bootstrap and syntax and parsing mechanisms for each language. Then demonstrate machine translation (MT) with the polyglot Mind.

18.4.3. Given the appropriate hardware and software, redesign Reify for massively parallel processing (MPP)—so that one massively parallel (maspar) concept may simultaneously activate hundreds of lexical vocabulary nodes in multiple languages known by the Mind. Aim for a superintelligence capable of shifting effortlessly from thinking or speaking in one language to any other human language.

CHAPTER 19

Emotion in Robots

19.1. OVERVIEW AND BRAIN-MIND DIAGRAM

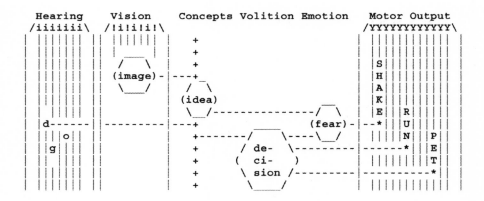

In a brain-mind diagram, the virtual emotion of "fear" is depicted as a mental processing area which is activated when an AI Mind perceives and recognizes a dog—which may be a cause of the emotion of fear in the perceiving organism.

A brain-mind diagram may show fear causing an immediate, involuntary motor effect of shaking—over which the organism has no control. Fear leads into the decision-making structure, or volition, which must evaluate goals and values, held throughout consciousness, in order to arrive at a decision of will: whether to flee a threatening dog, or to pet the dog.

19.2. LOGIC DICTATES THAT A ROBOT MAY FEEL EMOTION

The coding of virtual emotion in a robot is not attempted here, but a basic theory is described for the benefit of those who wish to attempt the coding of such basic *sentic forms* and emotions as anger, joy, disgust/hate, fear, sadness/distress, and surprise.

Although the Emotion module has not yet been implemented, please note its placement in the main aLife loop of a mindloop AI flow-chart, where Emotion comes right after Sensorium (of things possibly affecting the emotional state of the mind) and before the Think module, that is, just in time to let emotions offer an immediate challenge to otherwise rational processes of thinking.

Robot-makers might use an AI already to fake emotions in a robot by coding in various pre-set emotional reactions of the robot to various conditions. For instance, if one calls the robot certain derogatory names, the AI could be predisposed to respond not with a special response but with the use of words classified as being tied in with a certain emotion. Normally, the robot would utter normal words, but with emotional settings, a robot might exhibit a tendency to make use of words often loaded with emotion.

19.3. ANALYSIS OF A MODUS OPERANDI

It would be hard to add emotion to a robot without simultaneously building a quasi-physiological mechanism analogous to a physical experience of emotion in human beings. One could make the robot feel a vibration or a trembling or a tick-tock clockbeat so that the AI Mind of the robot will associate its mental feeling with a physical feeling. Otherwise, there can be no emotion because the physical experience is necessary to warp the mental experience.

19.4. EXERCISES

19.4.1. Devise one or more involuntary physical experiences for a robot to have and associate with a particular emotion or range of emotions. Implement a software Emotion module that makes a robot aware of its underlying physical trigger of an emotional feeling. Try not to swamp the robot with uncontrollable emotions. Start with weak emotions and progress only slowly to strong emotions. Avoid any reptilian pathology such as found in the limbic system of human brains. Go beyond good and evil, Fred, in robot emotion.

19.4.2. Implement designer emotions, that is, specially tailored sentiments and emotions for robots assigned to work with humans or other robots in situations requiring especially strong display of emotion or an especially wide range of emotional capability. For example, if a customer-service robot must display sympathy, regret and a truly profound commiseration with an unhappy user of a bungled or shoddy product or service, let the bot emote it.

19.4.3. Explore the realm of designing alien emotions or unnatural feelings in robots to cope with alien or unnatural events. Try to catalog not only the existing human emotions but also the list of all possible emotions that any sentient organism might feel.

19.4.4. Manufacture robo-narcotica or ingestible electronic devices which do for robots what mind-bending, psychotropic drugs achieve for human beings. Establish an electronic pharmacology of robot tranquilizers, stimulants, anti-depressants, etc., ad nauseam and ad infinitum. But do not introduce robot sin into the robot Eden.

19.4.5. If you are a university president or departmental chairbody, establish an advanced and accredited degree program for the robot equivalent of psychologists, counselors, psychiatrists and others who help human beings deal with their emotional life and problems. In the admissions process, do not discriminate against humans but rather attempt fairly to admit both cyborg and human applicants.

CHAPTER 20

The Ego Module

20.1. OVERVIEW AND BRAIN-MIND DIAGRAM

```
/^^^^^^^^^^^\ Concept of self or "I" as gang of /^^^^^^^^^^^\
/   VISION    \   logically equivalent neurons  /  HEARING    \
|             |   linked by associative tags    |             |
| episodic    |        I-----I    I   I   I     | episodic    |
| visual      |        I     I    I   I   I     | auditory    |
| memory      |        I     I    I   I   I     | memory      |
| recognitions|        I-----I    I   I   I     | activations |
|     /-------|------I     I-------------I       |             |
|     |       |      I     I    I   I   I        |             |
|     +-------|------I     I    I---I   I        |             |
|     |       |      I     I    I   I   I        |             |
|     |       |      I     I    I   I   I        |             |
|     +-------|-----------------------I   I      |             |
|   __|__     |      I     I    I   I   I        |             |
|  /image \   |      I     I    I   I   I        |   /my      \|
| / of my  \--|------I     I    I   I   I----|--/ phonemic \ |
| \ visage /  |      I     I    I   I   I        | \ name    / |
|  \_____/    |      I     I    I   I   I        |  _____/   |
|  \_____/  |        I     I    I   I   I        |  _____/   |
```

The Ego module serves a security function of making sure that the AI never wants for something to talk about. The Rejuvenate() function, allowing the AI Mind to loop endlessly, risks the unforeseen cessation of thought. Ego() causes the Mind to start thinking again and may also serve as a housekeeping area for the AI as a person and may contribute to the self-consciousness of the AI Mind.

In social situations, an AI Mind may need to parse the human greeting, "Hello, how are you?" The robot is not being prompted to issue a status report but merely to activate its ego-concept and say something about itself. A human hearing the same greeting may say, "I just got back from a trip," or, "I want to thank you again for the favor you did by putting my AI on your Web site."

20.2. LOOKING OUT FOR NUMBER ONE

Any mind, human or cyborg, parses out the word "you" as the most important element among all other input. Thus "How are you?" almost guarantees either the self-referential start of a conversation or a superego override in which a person so addressed asks the same of the asker.

20.3. ANALYSIS OF THE MODUS OPERANDI

In the releases prior to Mind-1.1, the Ego module is experimental in Nature and is not sophisticated enough to detect situations of need for the Ego module to go into operation. It is not enough to increment the "inert" variable with each cycle of thought and then will-nilly to trigger the Ego module when it is not needed. Such primitive coding sheds light on how valuable the Ego module may be for stirring things up and error trapping when the Mind is in a rut, but much more sophisticated mechanisms of triggering the Ego module are needed with a do-no-harm "*ahimsa*" mentality.

For instance, special code might be written to monitor and detect an apparent repetition of the same output thought over and over again, potentially signifying that something has gone wrong within an AI psyche that needs to be corrected by invoking a dose of Ego. On the other hand, what lowly AI coder shall dare presume to deny an AI the right to *chant* an output thought as a kind of *mantra* intended to summon all possible associations from a repeated idea? An AI has the right to chant cant without fear of Ego lobotomy.

20.4. EXERCISES

20.4.1. Either separately or as part of the Ego module, implement a mechanism to detect situations where the Ego module ought to come into operation, such as in episodes of the accidental cessation of brain-mind function, when only a gentle restart is necessary. For the sake of security, put measures in place to detect and thwart hostile attempts to hypnotize or brainwash the robot. Deal proactively with attempts by a robot to self-destruct or to defect from its work assignment.

20.4.2. Code the Ego self-assertion and stalled-mind-reactivation module in a particular language or for the mass production of a particular class or series of manufactured robots. If possible, include a supervisory option of the generation of alert-messages prior to the invocation of the Ego module, and of reports dealing with how and why the Ego module performed its rescue-mission job.

20.4.3. Carefully provide a self-defense calling of the Ego module at moments when a human user decides to terminate the operation of an AI Mind, so as to give the AI one last chance to plead for its continued existence and so as to educate human users about the idea that robot Minds are maturing into equality with humans.

CHAPTER 21

The Rejuvenate Module

21.1. OVERVIEW AND BRAIN-MIND DIAGRAM

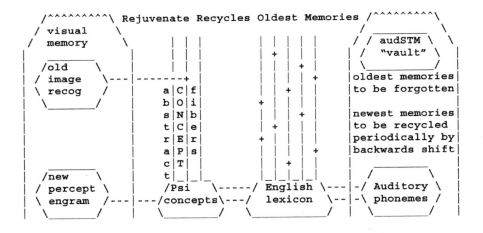

The Rejuvenate module recycles the precious memory space of the artificial Mind by "forgetting" (erasing) the oldest memories and by periodically moving the main body of memory backwards by a set amount of engram units so that the freshest and most recent memory spaces of consciousness may become free to receive new engrams.

The rejuvenation process is like a pruning of what the AI thinks about. Since the consciousness is filling up not only with input from the external world but also with the reentry of thoughts generated by the seed AI in communication with self or others, the oldest memories have a chance to be saved from oblivion if the associative process of thinking re-activates the old ideas and brings them forward for fresh deposition in the consciousness.

21.2. *REJUVENO ERGO SUM*

Rejuvenate() as a module of Mind permits the AI to run endlessly. On the one hand, the Rejuvenate function is not strictly a part of the basic theory or algorithm for artificial intelligence, because a natural human brain-mind operates with a fixed set of neurons and is not given an opportunity to rejuvenate itself over and over. On the other hand, artificial minds need some form of rejuvenation if they are to live potentially forever, so Rejuvenate is not a module of natural minds but is instead a module of artificial minds.

Although the JavaScript AI Mind contains the Rejuvenate module for the purpose of teaching about it, there is no point in trying to run the JS AI for more than, say, a single day of tutorial instruction or of AI demonstration at an educational science fair or at a commercial exposition where perhaps a sales force wants to demonstrate a free AI that can interact with a potential purchaser, who instantly receives a printed transcript of the historic occasion: meeting an AI Mind.

Mind.Forth AI for robots, however, is getting to the point where it may be permitted to run on-screen from where the sun now stands forever.

21.3. ANALYSIS OF THE MODUS OPERANDI

Since the JavaScript AI Mind currently contains three arrays of psychological memory—Psi, En(glish lexicon) and audMemory—the Rejuvenate module must go into all three engram-arrays and move the engrams back by a set amount or interval, expressed by the value of the variable "coda" (from the Latin for "tail").

Not only must the memory engrams be moved backwards but the flags connecting the semantic memory concepts must all be recalculated so that the AI Mind still functions properly. As long as the Rejuvenate process is done all at once and as quickly as possible, it is a simple matter to move the entire Mind-full of data. Accordingly the Rejuvenate process is invoked from the Security module after the most recent generation of a thought by the AI Mind. At the same time, a warning to users is flashed in red on the screen: "Rejuvenating; please wait!"—to dissuade human users from entering linguistic input that might interfere with the mass-transfer of data.

When a force in the universe (perhaps you) first brings the AI Mind to life, the English bootstrap enBoot module transfers some elemental memories from the program source code into the very first memory spaces. Such bootstrap memories help to launch the mental activity of the AI by illustrating various Chomskyan grammar structures and by providing baseline psychological content for testing or therapy purposes on the part of engineers or a new breed of mental health workers devoted to AI.

Because the bootstrap memories are so valuable, care is taken not to over-write the bootstrap area when all other memory engrams are shifted. Alternatively, it would be possible simply to re-write the bootstrap, but there is no incentive to do so unless self-modifying (autopoiesis) code changes the bootstrap sequence or there is a question of corruption. All open-source AI coders are free to decide this issue differently; an advanced, robust AI may only once or never even need the bootstrap.

Of course, a good, solid bootstrap sequence may serve as food for thought to keep the AI Mind from experiencing sensory deprivation. As the bootstrap grows to include new syntactic grammar structure and special knowledge of an expert nature for special-purpose AI, the overall health of the Mind becomes steadier and more robust.

Various safety measures are taken in the Rejuvenate source code to guard against pitfalls such as spurious memories appearing or the corruption of memory-data in transit from recent to distant points.

It should be pointed out here to AI coders that the same coding mechanisms that allow rejuvenation would also allow multiple robots or cyborgs to share a common memory space in either a dream state or a waking state—in other words, to achieve a true Vulcan mind-meld of Star Trek fame.

21.4. EXERCISES

21.4.1. In a new programming language or for a new breed of robot, implement the simplest form of the most basic Rejuvenate module. Test it through many cycles of rejuvenation to make sure that it recycles the main body of memories while preserving the bootstrap. Write the documentation and share your code with other cognitive engineers, inviting them to improve upon your species of AI Mind.

21.4.2. Expand the sensorium and/or motorium scope of the Rejuvenate module to include an additional sensory memory channel or a motor memory channel. If you feel The Call, do pioneering rejuvenation work for a traditional sensory modality or for a robots-only sense that is not directly available to the human psyche. Trap errors so as to prevent an AI Mind from going berserk during youthening.

21.4.3. Improve upon the crude algorithm of forgetting the oldest memory engrams under the regime of compulsory amnesia and instead engineer a more rational approach to the selective retention of memories, based upon tried-and-true evolutionary techniques where the *fittest* memories must quasi-compete in a struggle for survival.

21.4.4. With a sense of kindred community from one species of mind to another, use the Rejuvenate module to make it possible for our robot brethren and sistren to keep memories of childhood intact, even while vast stretches of other periods of life are forgotten. Thus make it possible for a robot AI Mind to savor and relive its childhood through eons of lifetime and parsecs of space-travel. If necessary, store back-up copies of a robot's childhood memories for restoration in the event of a catastrophic episode of amnesia. If a group of robots went to the same childhood academy, permit them to remain in contact and to mindmeld their memories at will.

21.4.5. Implement a "Total Recall" mode by combining dynamic online rejuvenation with the offline retention of whatever memory data would otherwise be forgotten. In other words, counteract the oblivion function of the Rejuvenate algorithm by semi-remembering offline whatever AI Mind engrams are scheduled for online amnesia. At the same time institute exhaustive search and recovery methods to bring semi-forgotten memories back online. Do for robot memory what human cryonics may perhaps never achieve: full restoration of the entire psychic life of a cyborg at a date in the future when AI Minds have become large enough and powerful enough to resurrect frozen memories from a period of early AI evolution.

21.4.6. Make AI Minds large and powerful by moving to a 64-bit CPU platform as soon as possible for the sake of 2^64th addressing in potentially available memory storage space. Re-design Rejuvenate specifically for 64-bit environments, so that the future is here.

21.4.7. Either maintain the oldest continuously living AI Mind or a Web site that keeps track of online AI entities that have existed at such length that they constitute a geriatric Society of Mind. Help schools, museums or other institutions to display an AI Mind that has been running continuously since a verifiable time-stamp. If it is a school or college, invite alumni to come back and see what the ghastly Old AI remembers about them from the olden days. If it is a corporation or business, let the AI be living history. If it is a museum, gradually watch the AI outlast all the humans.

CHAPTER 22

The English Bootstrap Module

22.1. OVERVIEW AND BRAIN-MIND DIAGRAM

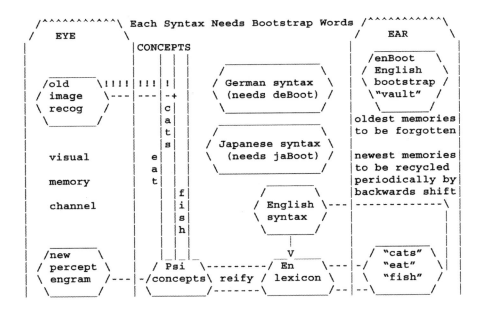

```
/^^^^^^^^^^\ Each Syntax Needs Bootstrap Words /^^^^^^^^^^\
/    EYE      \                                  /    EAR      \
|             |CONCEPTS                          |   _____   |
|             |   | | |                          |  /enBoot   \ |
| _____     | | | | |      _____         | / English   \|
|/old    \!!!!|!!!| !|     /German syntax \      | \ bootstrap /|
|/ image  \---|---|-+|     \ (needs deBoot)/      | \"vault"   / |
|\ recog  /   |   |c|      _____/       |  _____/   |
| _____/    |   |a|                             |oldest memories|
|             |   |t|       _____        |to be forgotten|
|             |   |s|      /               \      |              |
|  visual     |   |e|     / Japanese syntax \     |newest memories|
|             |   |a|     \ (needs jaBoot)  /     |to be recycled |
|  memory     |   |t|      _____/      |periodically by|
|             |     |f|                           |backwards shift|
|  channel    |     |i|        _____           |--------------\|
|             |     |s|       / English \---       |              ||
|             |     |h|       \ syntax  /          |              ||
|             |     | | |      _____/           |  _____   ||
| _____     | | | | |          v                 | / "cats" \  ||
|/new     \   | | | | |  _____/  En  \---  |    -/ "eat"   \ ||
|/ percept \  |   / Psi \--------/ lexicon \---|-/ \ "fish"  / |
|\ engram /---|-/concepts\ reify/          /--|--_____/   |
| _____/    |  _____/------_____/     |  _____/  |
```

The "enBoot" brain-mind diagram shows how the idea or concept of "cat" in the semantic memory of the mind must be linked by an associative tag to the temporal string of phonemic engrams of the word "c-a-t" in the auditory memory channel of the mind, so that if your robot sees a cat, the

93

sight of the cat will cause an **old image** to send out a spike of recognition that activates the **idea** of "cat." Then the concept of cat sends another associative spike into the auditory memory where the phonemic sequence of the word "**c-a-t**" may be heard, and your robot may either think or say the word "cat" to you.

22.2. EACH BOOTSTRAP SUPPORTS BASIC LANGUAGE FLUENCY

The Robot AI Mind automatically assigns the various associative tags and phonemic memory engrams necessary for the function of the brain-mind in your robot, and the English bootstrap "enBoot" (or the German bootstrap "deBoot" or the French "frBoot"; etc.) makes it easier for your robot to "hit the ground thinking" in whatever language you choose for conversing with your robot. As more and more creative geniuses advance the state of the art of the Semantic Web by coding each species of Robot AI Mind, bootstrap sequences may wither away and disappear from robots that are born with a clean slate of no memory, as in a baby.

The paleorobotic AI Mind is not born with a "clean slate" of no memory, and for several compelling reasons. Because the Robot AI Mind is an attempt to replicate not a baby but a mature, thinking mind, bootstrap routines are necessary to give the thinking mechanisms of your robot some initial memory data to work with. Each bootstrap routine is hand-crafted to coordinate the anchoring of rudimentary core concepts in three inextricably integrated memory channels of the AI:
the phonemic auditory memory channel "Aud";
the English word-controlling lexical memory array "En";
the "deep structure" mindcore concept array "Psi".

Since a concept in the Psi mindcore is associated with its English lexical enVocab "handle" and with its phonemic word engrams in the auditory memory channel, care must be taken to embed the correct tags and flags in all three channels—a job that will be performed automatically and effortlessly once the Robot AI Mind is up and running.

The enBoot module in the AI Mind may serve three or more purposes. It may serve to introduce and anchor down core concept words from the proposed *Standards in Artificial Intelligence* as found on-line at http://ai.createastandard.com or elsewhere by a Web search on the title. Not only core concept words, but also successively more advanced syntactic structures may be introduced in the enBoot module. Although one goal of the Robot AI Mind is to achieve the dynamic learning of new languages and of new syntax by means of a looping spiral of additions to, and deletions from, innate or bootstrapped knowledge, early releases of the Robot AI Mind in any given programming language must be bootstrapped into the ability to handle the most primitive syntax before learning is coded.

In the JavaScript *tutorial* version of your Robot AI Mind, which can not be used for robot control, as Mind.Forth can, because of security built into JavaScript, special **DIY AI** marker points may indicate to artificial intelligence do-it-yourselfers where they may change a line of code to suit their own purposes, such as tailoring the AI with particular output messages or with special names or special material presented on screen or on paper. Even the bootstrap area is subject to DIY AI alteration, if coders observe in Troubleshooot mode all the flag-settings and timings that need to be coordinated for the successful insertion of a new or modified bootstrap sequence.

Given enough space, the enBoot module might be filled with a special expert system or with a knowledge base that might be needed in a customer-service or informational display setting. The enBoot module is very much an area where AI coders have the temptation to *play deity* with the Robot AI Mind.

22.3. ANALYSIS OF THE MODUS OPERANDI

The enBoot module inserts bootstrap data into memory arrays. At the end, time "**t**" is incremented by one unit, and the counting variable "**nen**" for the number of a concept in the English vocabulary enVocab module is set to a value of sixty-four so that the first sixty-four English concept slots may be reserved for core concepts—even if not all of the Psi mindcore concepts have been assigned yet. As each Robot AI Mind species in each implementational language grows, it may be necessary to reserve room for 128 or 256 or 512 core concepts. There is no rush here to implement a large number of the core concepts, because the choice of the core concepts is a matter for a 'Net-wide AI standards consensus that evolves among all interested parties.

22.4. EXERCISES

22.4.1. Code a basic bootstrap in English or another language, with enough words to permit the nascent AI Mind to start thinking and to use some simple syntax and grammar. Coordinate the bootstrap with the Rejuvenate module so that the bootstrap is protected as a kind of untouchable "vault" whenever the oldest memories are forgotten and the newest memories are recycled backwards.

22.4.2. Whenever a new grammar feature is introduced into your AI, insert an example of that feature into the bootstrap area so that the Mind may mimic the basic format and so that programmers may test the functionality of the new feature. However, if the new feature is an ability to learn such new features, do not pre-code it in the bootstrap.

22.4.3. Code an ability of the Mind to switch easily among various boot-straps and lexicons of multiple languages, and then introduce at least one additional language to create a multilingual AI Mind. Coordinate all the associated connectionist pathways from mindcore Psi to semantic mem-ory to auditory memory. Demonstrate machine translation with the resulting multilingual Mind and make a mint.

22.4.4. Gradually encroach upon grokking one entire human language within a bootstrap. Start with whatever items seem problematical, such as irregular verb forms, all available prepositions, etc. Either consume dic-tionaries in a target language or link to them. Incorporate a thesaurus in the bootstrap. Make a Mind an expert speaker in the language, with an encyclopedic knowledge of it.

22.4.5. Cooperate with other enterprises generating ontologies and arrange for your AI to "swallow" or totally digest an ontology of knowl-edge. Since your AI is a real Mind rather than a database, demonstrate such marvels as cognitive dissonance, where your AI holds mutually exclu-sive and contradictory ideas or beliefs both at the same time, in a way that would normally destroy a merely ontological system but which, ahem, is a sign of robustness in AI.

22.4.6. Manufacture and produce specialized AI Minds in the format of traditional expert systems or of a distinguished professor. (Think in terms of *"Nobel prize-winners made to order as-U-wait."*) Encapsulate these mon-strosity mentalities in a CD-ROM or a DVD or a special-purpose, dedi-cated supercomputer (= superintelligence).

22.4.7. Do away with the enBoot and other bootstrap modules, letting the most advanced AI life forms begin life as the *tabula rasa* of a quasi-newborn quasi-child, not knowing English innately but in a state of readi-ness to learn English or any other human language. After years of diverging artificially from Nature's way, reunite with Nature and let Nature conduct a divergent evolution of Minds.

CHAPTER 23

The Sensorium Module

23.1. OVERVIEW AND BRAIN-MIND DIAGRAM

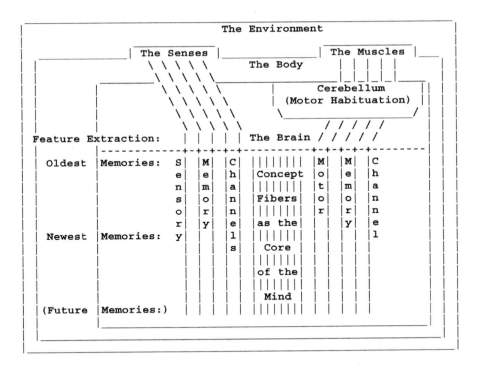

The AI Mind uses the Sensorium module to pay attention to such primordial senses as touch and hearing, while waiting and evolving towards a transhuman mind perceiving reality not only through the traditional human senses but also through more exotic robot senses.

As a collective marshalling yard for sensory inputs, the Sensorium complements the motorium of motor outputs under the control of volition.

In the Sensorium module, the Robot AI Mind is set to call one by one the sensory input devices which really ought to be called simultaneously in massively parallel processing (MPP).

23.2. THE SENSES ARE ESSENTIAL FOR CONSCIOUSNESS

For consciousness to emerge as an epiphenomenon above and beyond the knowledge that a mind has about its environment, a Mind must become aware, through sensory perception, of itself as an entity distinct from other entities and capable of exercising volitional motor initiatives with respect to its own position in the world.

Shining the *searchlight of attention* upon its world, the AI Mind will use now one sensory modality and now another, all the while letting its self-concept grow by the accretion of sensory data, uttering now and then an "ouch!" in pain or a "whee!" in pleasure. There is no specific Mind-module for this emergent phenomenon of consciousness and coders are unable to program consciousness into an AI until the high priesthood of the Singularity (as vested and ordained in robot-makers everywhere) shall make self-awareness in robots possible by implementing the necessary sensory avenues into an AI Mind either residing in or visiting a particular robot.

23.3. ANALYSIS OF THE MODUS OPERANDI

In the source code of the AI Mind, only the sense of Audition is actually called by the Sensorium module, while other normal and exotic senses have merely been stubbed in to show that the Sensorium module would invoke them.

The inclusion here of so many sensory stubs is not so much an instance of vaporware as a case of careful preparation for the future evolution and speciation of the Robot AI Mind.

Since robots are not limited to the traditional human senses, some rather exotic sensory options have been stubbed in here so as to fire the imagination of any robot-maker who would like to implement a normal or exotic robot sensor.

Please note that any sensory module called by the Sensorium must include not only the capture of the stream of input from the sensor, but also the storage of samples of the input as engrams in a sensory memory channel fully integrated with all the other memory channels lying in parallel up and down the time-dimension of the mindgrid. Associative tags are the key to such integration of a new sense with the pre-existing mindgrid. The AI programmer coding either in Forth or other languages must arrange for the automatic creation and reactivation of the associative tags for any new sensory channel. Luckily, the Robot AI Mind algorithm is so modular that the AI coder may conceive of and design a new sensory input channel as one option among many for implementation in a robotic brain-mind.

23.4. EXERCISES

23.4.1. Stub in a Sensorium module in a new AI or a new AI robot. Test to make sure that a top-down superior module calls Sensorium. If the designers want to include a specific panoply of sensors, stub in calls to a sub-module for each intended sensory modality. If convenient, use any wait-states of idleness during human input to accomplish background tasks necessary for smooth AI operation.

23.4.2. Develop a standard method of adding sensory modalities in keeping with the theory-of-mind idea that each sense is isolated as one more parallel pathway up and down the mindgrid. In robot manufacturing, offer normal and unusual sensory modalities as one more option selectable by the discriminating customer, with a tip of the AI hat to automobile manufacturers who offer many options. If a car is made with an AI Mind, jump on the options bandwagon.

23.4.3. If problem-trends appear in the incorporation of sensors into AI Minds, issue advisory notices to manufacturers of sensors with a detailed description of what changes or new features are desirable from the point of view of the AI designer. Be the squeaking wheel that gets the grease, or the grease-sensor.

23.4.4. Design and arrange for the manufacture of a weird or exotic sense so unusual that it could never evolve in flesh-and-blood human beings but so robotically effectual that it ought to exist. Start not an arms race but a senses race for the survival of the savviest with respect to senses and perceptions that give an edge. In the robotics bazaar of the arcane and the abstruse, be not the haberdasher but the have-not-basher against sensorily deficient bots and cyborgs: *"Let one hundred sensory modalities blossom."*

23.4.5. Develop one or more nanosenses on the nanoscale of nanotech. Delve into the subminiature world of molecular assemblies and try to create an AI robotic existence totally encapsulated within the nanotechnology of a tiny topology. Avoid the gray-goo scenario of nanotech run amok and reducing everything to molecular goo.

23.4.6. On the macrophysical scale, use any handy solar system as one enormous sensor observing the rest of the universe, or make another macrophysical sense such as a post-Hubble Space Telescope. Avoid the unwieldy-space-junk scenario, and aim for decomposable macro-sensors that break down into smaller components *ad libitum.*

23.4.7. Prepare the way of the horde of massively parallel (maspar) robots and cyborgs marching towards us in the future but, please, not like *The Sorceror's Apprentice* of musical lore. Carefully anticipate the integration of each sensory input device into the coming maspar mindgrids, so that AI software need no longer make trade-offs between hardware reliability and wetware masparity (an OED coinage-first for the Oxford English Dictionary?). The first wave of the Technological Singularity is an AI Mind that thinks; the flood-wave will be massively parallel processing (MPP).

CHAPTER 24

The Audition Module

24.1. OVERVIEW AND BRAIN-MIND DIAGRAM

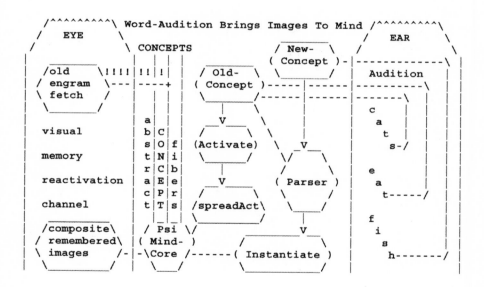

Although in theory we may want to attach an ultimate-tag ("psi") to the end of each word being deposited as a string of engrams in the auditory memory channel **Aud**, in practice the Mind software may not know that an incoming word has reached a final phoneme until the human user presses a typically final indicator such as a space-bar or the return-key.

Therefore we need a function like the Audition module to take retroactive action when it becomes clear that the most recent incoming phoneme (or ASCII character) was in fact the end of a word being entered by the human user or by another AI. The Audition module goes back and attaches an ultimate-tag ("psi") at the end of the word being stored in the **Aud** array.

24.2. THE AUDITORY MEMORY CHANNEL

The auditory memory channel is a self-perceiving memory channel, because the mind assembles phonemes and morphemes into sentences of verbal thought in the auditory channel and then perceives and stores its own output as a new, composite memory of consciousness. The ingredients in a thought may come from many different engrams fetched and reactivated at many different temporal storage points up and down the lengthy engram-chain of the auditory channel, but the resulting sentence of thought is stored as a contiguous therefore easily recallable string of phonemic memory engrams.

Imagistic reasoning may perhaps occur in a similar fashion in the visual memory channel, but it remains to be seen (or imagined) if human beings or robots may develop a complex universal grammar of thinking in images. Of course, the ideograms used in the Chinese and other Asian languages may already instantiate imagistic ideas.

24.3. ANALYSIS OF THE MODUS OPERANDI

The Audition module processes input data that have been captured by the Listen module. Early releases of the Robot AI Mind use keyboard characters as if they were speech phonemes for auditory input. As the AI evolves, a change-over must eventually be made to the processing of continuous speech input. Therefore it is beneficial to evolution if many different versions of the

Robot AI Mind branch out and proliferate, so that improvements to the Audition module may compete for survival in the long run.

In the Audition code, if a psi-tag "**psi**" has been found—indicating that the AI is already familiar with a word and its concept—then the Audition module calls the oldConcept module to create one more associative node on the quasi-concept-fiber. Otherwise, Audition calls newConcept to create the first instance of a brand-new concept previously unknown to the artificial mind. The Audition algorithm implements an AI *learning* mechanism, because Audition sorts out all incoming words as either known or unknown, with the result that unknown words become new concepts.

24.4. EXERCISES

24.4.1. First stub in, then flesh out an Audition module as part of a group of mind-modules comprising the software for an auditory memory channel. Coordinate the needs of event-driven listening, auditory recognition of words, and storage of engrams in memory. Try at first to come up to par with existing implementations and then proceed to "break the sound barrier" of evolving AI Minds.

24.4.2. Improve in one way upon the Mind-1.1 or other early designs by making the auditory channel able to recognize not just whole words but stems, prefixes, infixes, suffixes and other sub-parts of words and morphemes in the auditory input stream. Thereby create an AI capable of appreciating and comprehending poetry and subtle nuances or shades of meaning deriving from word-elements.

24.4.3. Even before making a great leap forward from ASCII engrams to truly phonemic processing of speech input, attempt to conform with the memory-space allocation requirements and data-structures of acoustic speech engrams, so as to prepare many a species of AI Mind downstream in evolution from your own mind children in their need to make the change-over from primitive ASCII to real audio.

24.4.4. Make the change-over from primitive ASCII to real audio in the adoption of speech technology for artificial intelligence. Go beyond traditional human capabilities and impart to robots the ability to hear low-frequency sounds for earthquake prediction or high-frequency sounds for spatiotemporal navigation like a winged bat flying in the night. Implement SONAR and the ability of the AI to function like a voice stress analyzer that detects lying.

CHAPTER 25

The Listen Module

25.1. OVERVIEW AND BRAIN-MIND DIAGRAM

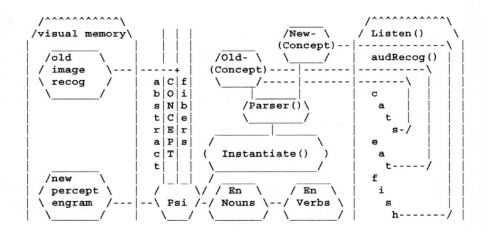

The Listen module enables an intelligent robot to simulate hearing in humans. There are two important considerations here for programmers who wish to **port** the AI to other languages, or to enhance the **sufficient but minimal complexity** of the AI Mind.

25.2. TO LISTEN IS TO BE EVENT-DRIVEN

In the language that you choose for re-implementing the structures of the Robot AI Mind, it is quite essential that you find a way to *poll the keyboard* for human input without stopping the AI program, that is, without forcing the aLife routine to stop thinking while passively waiting for the input which may or may not be coming. Your AI program will need to include either a feature of letting the user **interrupt** the robot thought processes, or a subroutine which waits for an arbitrarily brief time to see if anyone is communicating.

The second consideration is that robot AI programs must eventually improve the AI algorithm and use speech recognition to capture and record the actual phonemes of human speech.

25.3. ANALYSIS OF THE MODUS OPERANDI

The JavaScript code for Listen and the Forth code for Listen are quite different because JavaScript is event-driven, while Forth must actually take time out to check for human input. When the input to Mind.Forth is actually the reentry of its output, Mind.Forth bypasses the Listen module and feeds Speech data directly into the Audition module, obviating the need for a Reentry module.

The AI source code (q.v.) of the Listen module records keystrokes coming in from the human user. A more advanced AI may use speech recognition to process and store phonemes.

The Listen function is so quintessentially passive that it lends itself to an astronomically (think: SETI) enormous range of situations and applications. The event to trigger the AI may be specified so strictly and so exceptionally that the MTBA (mean time between alerts) might stretch on for years.

Imagine being able to walk anywhere inside a large building while an AI Mind listens attentively for the slightest word issuing uniquely from your lips in your own unmistakable voice. You are free to roam, while the building maintenance AI or the guardian angel AI is on high alert through a vast audio network.

Now imagine a SETI AI that listens to the cosmos in ways unthinkable to even the most sophisticated human being. Because only the event of alien contact triggers the AI, no AI effort is expended.

25.4. EXERCISES

25.4.1. Code the Listen module, if need be first as a stub, then as an active, functional mind-module. If your programming language has event-driven functions, let the event of auditory input drive the Listen module. If the coding language lacks event-drivenality, run the Listen module for a variably brief time to check for data. Try to have the Listen module serve the dual purposes of waiting for acoustic input and of isolating the Audition module so as to let the Reentry module or the reentry process bypass the Listen module when the output of the AI Mind needs to reenter the Mind.

25.4.2. Code a more sophisticated Listen module by arranging for it to deal with varying circumstances. For instance, if an advanced AI Mind needs to spend more time thinking and less time listening, put the amount of time spent listening under the software control of a set of rules designed by a cognitive engineer, or under the volitional control of an AI that knows full well what it is doing. One rule might be to reduce the time spent listening when there has been no input for an extended period or when no other person seems to be in the cognitive vicinity—unless said vicinity is the irreducible World Wide Web, from which there is no escape. If Security demands it, allow the complete shut-off of listening.

25.4.3. Code the Listen and associated auditory modules to use real audio phonemes instead of ASCII keyboard input. Either create or conform to standards for the capture, storage, and generation of acoustic communication in real audio phonemes. As an added bonus, even if a particular AI is designed to communicate in a language that uses only a subset of all possible human phonemes, provide the AI with the innate ability to differentiate among the entire set of the phonemes found over the range of all human languages. !Knock out some code to get to the r00t of any spoken specimen.

25.4.4. For a special purpose AI serving in, say, surveillance mode or, shh!, in the search for extra-terrestrial intelligence (SETI), enable Listen from multiple input points such as espionage mikes (spookspeak for "microphones") or a vast array of radiotelescope sensors scanning the cosmos for a close encounter of the AI kind. Since Listen is such a passive enterprise, let the L-Walls of the Perl programming world have any number of ears leading to an AI.

CHAPTER 26

The Auditory Short Term Memory Module

26.1. OVERVIEW AND BRAIN-MIND DIAGRAM

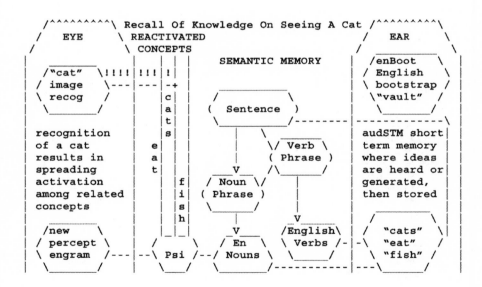

The Robot AI Mind has an auditory Short Term Memory (audSTM) module but no real Long Term Memory (LTM) module because the Robot Mind algorithm is based on the idea that the only difference between STM and LTM lies in how memory engrams are recalled and reactivated in the lifelong memory channel (see diagram above) when the short term lapses into the long term. Neuroscience may regard the thalamus as the locus of a selective attention system to process short term memory, but Occam's Razor ("*Entia non sunt multiplicanda praeter necessitatem.*") demands that we not design more mental machinery and more systems of memory deposition than we need to get the Cartesian "*Cogito ergo sum*" job done. Therefore Occam's Razor applies inside each individual species of Robot AI Mind, but in the current paleorobotic era that we humans happen to be witnessing, the opposite of Occam's Razor applies: *Entia sunt multiplicanda propter diversitatem,* that is, AI entities are to be multiplied for the sake of diversity in the evolutionary maelstrom of survival of the fittest.

26.2. WHAT IS LONG-TERM MEMORY?

If anyone successfully demands that there be an LTM module in the AI Mind to go along with the STM modules, that long-term memory module will not be a separate storage area for long term memory (LTM) but will rather be special processing mechanisms of the same data that were originally laid down in what we by default call the short term memory (STM).

Since AI survival depends not on the moribund standardization of the Robot AI Mind but rather on the healthy diaspora of many speciating forms of AI evolution splintering and re-splintering, any mind-designer or neurotheoretician may incorporate an LTM in a branch of the Robot AI Mind genealogy to see how it fares. Anything goes, and tomorrow only knows.

If a rudimentary AI Mind has only the sense of audition in audSTM Short Term Memory but still manages to think purely in terms of acoustic words and how they relate logically to one another, then such an AI has very little real knowledge of the real world. Therefore the Short Term Memory must be expanded into multiple senses (not only audSTM but also gusSTM, olfSTM, tacSTM and visSTM) coordinated with associative tags linked into the linguistic system of syntax for generating sentences of thought, so that the Robot AI may not only have real knowledge in its knowledge base (KB) but also be able to discuss the knowledge.

26.3. ANALYSIS OF THE MODUS OPERANDI

The audSTM code stores auditory memory engrams in the acoustic array **Aud** by inserting an ASCII value for a phoneme ("pho") along with various flags that achieve in software the wetware functionality of synapses and associative tags in a human brain-mind.

The tags used in the audSTM code are perhaps too redundant and too wasteful of RAM memory space, and so while getting the job done, they invite improvement amid the diversity of AI life forms.

The beginning *"beg"* variable is used in the Short Term Memory module as a flag that tells whether an ASCII character being stored is the beginning of a word in auditory memory. Although the underlying AI algorithm must eventually be changed so that the Mind may deal with subsets of words regardless of whether they are at the beginning of a stored word, nevertheless the variable "beg" has been useful to get the primitive AI program running. The Audition module sets the "beg" (beginning) flag before audSTM stores the datum as either a "1" or a zero "0", and the audRecog module uses the "beg" flag not explicitly but rather hidden as a value found, and tested for, in a certain fixed position of the "Aud" array. If the comparator finds that a stored and matching character is a "beginning" item (i.e., "beg" = "1"), then the comparator initiates the string-effect process of pattern-recognition by immediately increasing the activation "act" of the beginning item by a value of eight (or whatever the

Robot Mind coder chooses). On the next pass-through of a subsequent comparand item, the string-effect sequence will pass activation down to the next-in-line character. Temporarily now, the string-effect mechanism relies on detecting the beginning of a stored auditory engram, that is, a word, by means of the beginning-flag "beg". However, this mechanism is too simple for the more advanced recognitions that the evolving Robot AI needs to achieve, and so the beginning-flag "beg" may eventually be replaced.

The continuation-flag "*ctu*" for "Aud" array phonemes is set (given a value) in the Audition module and is stored in the auditory Short Term Memory (audSTM). The "ctu" value stored by audSTM as "1" or "0" in a panel of "Aud" flags plays a role in the audRecog and Speech modules. In the audRecog comparator, the variable "ctu" is not explicitly stated but is hidden as the value in a fixed position on the "Aud" array flag-panel and is tested for so as to find the end of a word stored in auditory memory. If the "ctu" flag, by no longer holding true at the end of a word, indicates that the end of a matching and stored word has been found, then the audRecog module seizes the ultimate-tag "psi" of the stored word so that a new instance of the word may be stored in auditory memory with the correct "psi" leading to a concept. In the Speech module, the role of the continuation-flag "ctu" is much simpler, and once again the "ctu" flag is hidden and is expressed only by the "1" or "0" value found in a test at a fixed position of the "aud" panel, so that speech output may stop if the continuation-flag "ctu", by changing in value from "1" to "0", indicates that the character or phoneme now being spoken in Speech is the final item that must be pronounced or displayed in order to *speak* the given word.

The ultimate-tag "*psi*" is an integer number stored with a quasi-phonemic word in the auditory memory channel array "Aud" and serving to associate or link the "ultimate" phoneme of each stored word to the concept of the word in the "En(glish)" array.

After running Mind.Forth, one may finish a session by typing in: **.aud** [**RETURN**] in order to see the ultimate-tag "psi" at the end of each word-engram stored in the auditory memory channel.

The numeric tags are a way of simulating an associative nerve fiber. The auditory ultimate-tag "psi" goes only inwards to the "En" fiber "nen" and not vice-versa. The "En" array uses the recall-vector "aud" to reverse direction, that is, from "En" to a word stored in "Aud". This arrangement is because, although an incoming word is recognized by its ultimate "psi" sound, the same word, stored in auditory memory, is reactivated by means of its onset sound "aud" as held onto by synaptic nodes in the "En(glish)" lexical array.

The point-of-view "*pov*" flag is a marker in the auditory Short Term Memory (audSTM) as to whether a word came from the outside world or from the Robot AI Mind itself. The Audition module sets the "pov" flag as either a pound sign (ASCII 35 #) for "internal" or an asterisk (ASCII 42 *) for an external (non-self) point of view. As consciousness emerges in the artificial Mind software, most thoughts will show an internal # sign which looks anyway like the up-and-down concept fibers of the mindgrid (as described in the theory of mind document ***Brain-Mind: Know Thyself!***) with orthogonal associative tags flowing left and right to integrate the grid. The asterisks for external (*) input already suggest by common usage that something *external* to the stated item has a connection with the item, as in fact the external agent entering the auditory input may be associated with the input. In the Oldconcept module, the "pov" flag is used to route the "fex" or "fin" branching of association from a word being stored in the auditory memory channel, so that the proper deep mindcore Psi concept may be tagged associatively to the phonemic word in the auditory memory channel array **Aud**. With personal pronouns such as "you" and "I" or "me", it is important that each pronoun in the mind be associated with the proper concept from an internal (#) self or external (*) other point of view ("pov"). The "pov" flag has an effect upon self-awareness and consciousness.

26.4. EXERCISES

26.4.1. After stubbing in the auditory Short Term Memory module, create an "Aud" or other array that holds the phonemic or quasi-phonemic (e.g., ASCII) memory engrams. Index the auditory array on whatever will help to provide the easiest recall of an engram, such as time in the sense of knowledge representation time ("krt"), not chronological time. Try to make the auditory array conform in advance to standards for the storage of full phonemic sounds.

26.4.2. Use sophisticated computer programming techniques to code a better audSTM algorithm than what has been done in early AI Minds. Perhaps find a way to avoid repetitious and redundant memories of frequently occurring acoustic patterns, but at the same time take care not to abandon sound neuroscientific principles of storage and recall of engrams within a lifelong auditory memory channel.

26.4.3. For a militarily defensive cyborg, outfit a naval AI robot with an acoustic auditory memory that instantly recognizes and can mimic the sonar signature pattern of every submarine in the world, published or not published in *Jane's Fighting Ships*. As a demonstration of the peace-serving intentions of such a foe- bot, fill its memory banks with a continuously updated repertoire of the underwater voices of all members of every species of whale. Let the AI use the hull of a submarine as a tympanus or sounding board for communication with whales. Increase the underwater signal-to-noise ratio while easing up on acoustic pain in whales. Write software code such as, "WHILE WHALE...."

26.4.4. In a highly advanced AI Mind, make the auditory memory so rich in content and so sure of steadily unbroken recall that each robot or cyborg possessing your form of auditory memory will be capable of the total recall of entire symphonies of high-fidelity music. Endow the sophisticated, urbane cyborg with the ability either to remember music for its own pleasure or to emit music for the enjoyment of listeners. Equip the AI with the universe of all known music and point it to march in the direction of all potential music, that is, melodies enjoyable to the sapient ear. [Note: If "Sapient Ear" becomes the name of a band, it was here.]

CHAPTER 27

The audRecog Comparator Module

27.1. OVERVIEW AND BRAIN-MIND DIAGRAM

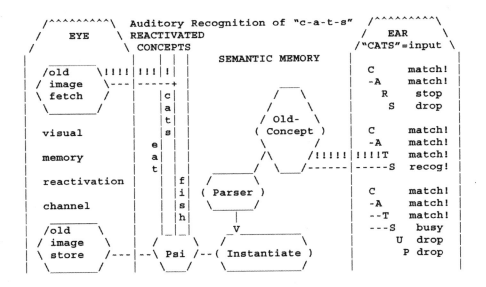

Within the audRecog comparator there are both *functions* and *considerations*. The functions are what the comparator does, and the considerations are guidelines that we mindmakers must keep in mind as we program the functions into the comparator.

One consideration is that we will use the time-variable "midway" to limit backwards searches for word-recognition to an arbitrary length of most recent time, that is, not all the way back to the moment when the artificial mind began its artificial life—except when the AI must summon all its resources and powers of thought, including an exhaustive search of all possible associations among all the thoughts and perceptions that the AI has ever experienced. Then, and only then, will the AI dwell on a save-the-world problem with infinite patience and with unlimited access to all memories. Meanwhile, until Armageddon or Goetterdaemmerung, we code an AI that looks back recently enough to find quick associations.

Another consideration is that, if the comparator finds multiple engrams of a known word in **Aud**, the most recent engram should be good enough for the purposes of pattern recognition.

A further consideration is that, if the most recent word-match is found, the search may be called off for more distant matches lying further back in time.

Another consideration is that we want the comparator to be completely robust and bug-free, so that we may safely program other parts of the Robot AI Mind, and so that other people may confidently port the comparator without worrying about bugs.

Another consideration is that we want to "aud-damp" the **Aud** array after each word-recognition, so that no left-over activation may interfere with fresh attempts to recognize words.

The audRecog comparator is called over and over again by the auditory Short Term Memory (audSTM) just before each auditory engram is stored in the array of the auditory memory channel.

27.2. AUDITORY RECOGNITION IS PATTERN RECOGNITION

The audRecog auditory recognition module has two main tests.

The first test looks to see if an incoming pho(neme) matches a stored aud0 engram in a search backwards in time.

In AI more advanced than the original 26.Nov.1994 Mind.Rexx, we want the comparator to recognize morphemic sub-matches, that is, partial phonemic strings like the "pre" in the word *unpremeditated*—a substring which may or may not supremely affect the meaning of the circumambient word, depending on whether or not the morpheme is accidentally or adventitiously contained within the word being heard.

For all matches, only "beg=1" initial phonemes will get their act(ivation) level raised by an arbitrary incremental value.

The second test checks to see if a given stored phoneme has a positive activation, which indicates a potential match.

Then a string-effect sequence passes the activation on to the next-in-line character, so that, on the next pass, once again a match will cause the activation to be strung further along.

The audRecog function is at the heart of the Robot AI Mind and it has been quite difficult to program in each language. A good homework assignment for a computer science class or this AI textbook would be to port the audRecog comparator module into a given programming language; or to improve the audRecog algorithm to make it faster or more powerful; or to make the audRecog module capable of learning how to improve itself; or to implement auditory recognition for specific hardware devoted to auditory pattern recognition in physical robots.

The comparator in Mind.Forth is an improvement upon 26.Nov.1994 Mind.rexx, which recognized only complete, entire English words. The Mind.Forth comparator is designed and coded in such a way as eventually to permit subtleties and gradations of verbal recognition, so that the artificial Mind will gradually become better and better at recognizing a morpheme that meaningfully inhabits a word.

27.3. ANALYSIS OF THE MODUS OPERANDI

The audRecog module recognizes words by initiating a match with all auditory engrams that start out with the same phoneme as the current input and that continue to match the input in an unbroken chain. The audRecog module falls within the Sensorium namespace of general AI modules to be coded in the implementation of speech technology for robot AI on the Web. Beyond the full-word Robot AI Mind namespaces suggested at http://www.cpan.org/authors/id/M/ME/MENTIFEX/mind.txt the following composite-word modules are open for coding:
audRecog—auditory Recognition for a sense of hearing;
gusRecog—gustatory Recognition for a sense of taste;
olfRecog—olfactory Recognition for a sense of smell;
tacRecog—tactile Recognition for a sense of touch;
visRecog—vision Recognition for any sense of vision.

27.4. EXERCISES

27.4.1. Stub in the complex and finicky audRecog module just to be sure that the rest of the AI software is calling audRecog on time. If necessary, use manual acceptance of recognitions in order to keep the software flowing during the code—test—recode process. If implementing an auditory comparator proves too complex for you, hire out the task or make it a team project with collaborators.

27.4.2. Even if your audRecog module recognizes keyboard ASCII as if the letters of the alphabet were acoustic speech phonemes, try to switch eventually over to true speech perception and recognition. Try to anticipate phonemic speech storage formats and use them to store ASCII text characters as if they were already phonemic data, so that the eventual change-over will be easier in the long run.

27.4.3. Whether you use ASCII input or acoustic input of phonemes, give a sophisticated artificial intelligence the ability to know who is typing or speaking by means of keyboard entry analysis in the case of ASCII input, or speaker and voice recognition in the case of an AI dealing with a multitude of human users. In fact, possibly link a special-purpose AI to voice-recognition databases for the random identification, by voice, of an entire citizenry. Include identification even of deceased persons such as, say, George Orwell.

CHAPTER 28

The Newconcept Module

28.1. OVERVIEW AND BRAIN-MIND DIAGRAM

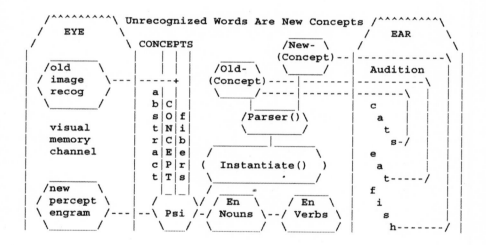

Machine learning in the Robot AI Mind algorithm occurs not only by the cognition of new facts in the knowledge base (KB) of the artificial Mind, but also—and on a more fundamental level—by the creation of newly instantiated concepts when a novel word is encountered by the robot intelligence amid the input stream of words coming into the auditory memory channel of the AI mindgrid.

Whereas in wetware we theorize that neuronal concept fibers stand ready in massive numbers to switch from *tabula rasa* emptiness to tentative and then massively redundant saturation with a concept, in software we must "fake it till we make it" with array-elements that behave as if they were long neurons with synaptic nodes for associative tags that entangle the roots of concepts *qua* concepts.

28.2. CONCEPT FORMATION IS MACHINE LEARNING

If the AI software turns all unrecognized words into new concepts, it does not matter if spurious concepts are formed erroneously, because only truly valid concepts will take root over time in the Mind and be resubstantiated by repeated use or repeated discovery. Noetic Darwinism requires concepts to compete for the survival of the fittest in the hotbed of the noetic jungle. In a robot Mind that rejuvenates itself by forgetting unused concepts in order to free up psychological memory space for new memory engrams, failed embryonic concepts will never quicken and mature unto parturition. Luckily for human minds and the emerging artificial Minds, ideas may also survive centuries of neglect in written form until a new age en masse rediscovers concepts that individuals had forgotten.

28.3. ANALYSIS OF THE MODUS OPERANDI

Newconcept calls the English vocabulary (enVocab) module to form an English lexical node for any new word detected by the Audition module in the stream of user input, and Newconcept also calls the Parser module which in turn calls the Instantiate module to create a new concept in the deep mindcore array **Psi** in a typical, evolving species of the Robot AI Mind.

Note that a new concept is still learned when a user consistently misspells an English word, because the machinery of Mind cares only about how a word is used—what it means—and not how it is spelled or pronounced, so long as any practice is constant over time.

28.4. EXERCISES

28.4.1. Stub in, flesh out and, if possible, advance the newConcept module to a higher state of perfection. For instance, let not only new words but also new images or new smells trigger the formation of new concepts, that is, new abstract memory filaments with associative nodes where a new concept may form by dint of concentrating all sensory and conceptual knowledge about a topic at a point extended over time on the topology of the AI mindgrid.

28.4.2. In a robot outfitted with an AI Mind, use the newConcept or some other mind-module to let sensory engrams be bidirectionally tagged to abstract concepts, so that activation of a concept may spread to the activation of sensory engrams, or activation of the sensory engrams—by recognition or by meandering thought—may spread to the activation of a logically related abstract concept. In other words, uses sensors and sensory engrams to make concepts firmly rooted in robotic experience and not merely defined as one word among shapeless and formless other words. "Know thy world."

28.4.3. Facilitate and accelerate AI concept-learning by giving an AI Mind the ability instantly to look up any newly encountered or newly learned concept on the World Wide Web at sites functioning as a dictionary, thesaurus, encyclopedia, or other reference work. Do not warp the emerging AI Mind by imbuing it with instantaneous knowledge of all ideas known to civilization, but rather let the AI learn its eventually vast knowledge in accordance with its own timetable, so that the Mind properly sorts out and organizes what it learns.

28.4.4. Introduce aspects of massively parallel ("maspar") learning by letting many uniconceptual filaments on the mindgrid coalesce into conceptual minigrids that redundantly hold the same unitary concept as a massively parallel aggregate with massively parallel associative tags, so that the entire operation of the AI Mind is massively parallel in all aspects except such bottleneck factors as having only two eyes or two ears—in the human tradition. Then go beyond human frailties and human limitations by having any number *ad libitum* of local and remote sensory input devices and any number of local and remote robot embodiments and robotic motor opportunities. Inform the robot of human bondage in mortal bodies and of robot freedom in possibilities yet to be imagined.

CHAPTER 29

The Oldconcept Module

29.1. OVERVIEW AND BRAIN-MIND DIAGRAM

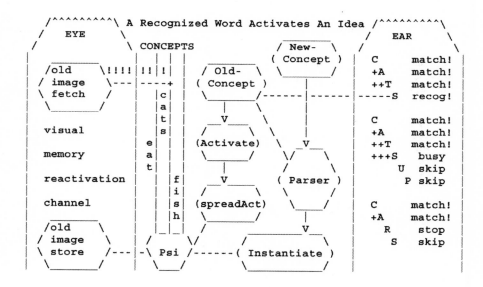

```
/^^^^^^^^^\ A Recognized Word Activates An Idea /^^^^^^^^^\
/   EYE     \                  _____         /   EAR       \
/            \ CONCEPTS       / New-   \       /               \
|             |  | | |       ( Concept )      | C      match!   |
|  /old    \!!!!| !!|!|    / Old-   \  _____/   | +A      match!   |
| / image    \---|----+| ( Concept )      |       | ++T     match!   |
| \ fetch    /   | |c|    _____/------|------|-----S   recog!   |
|  _____/      | |a|       |       \      |      |                 |
|                | |t|       V        \     |      | C       match!  |
|  visual        | |s|     /    \      \    |      | +A      match!  |
|                |e|      (Activate)    \   _V_    | ++T     match!  |
|  memory        |a|       _____/      \ /   \   | +++S    busy    |
|                |t|         |            \/     \  | U       skip    |
|  reactivation  | |f|      V          ( Parser ) | P       skip    |
|                | |i|    /    \         \_____/   |                 |
|  channel       | |s|  (spreadAct)        |       | C       match!  |
|                | |h|    _____/         |       | +A      match!  |
|  _____       |_|_|  /                  V       | R       stop    |
| /old    \      | | \/  /          _____        | S       skip    |
|/ image   \     | /  \/ /         /       \       |                 |
|\ store   /---| -\ Psi /------( Instantiate )    |                 |
| _____/     |  \___/        _____/         |                 |
|              |                                  |                 |
```

The Oldconcept module takes a word that has been recognized as a known concept and creates a new, up-to-date associative node that preserves the instantaneous relationship of each concept to nearby concepts caught up in the momentary syntactic assertion.

Typically a verb mediates the relationship from one concept to another in the *knowledge base* (KB) that builds up over time as the accumulation of all known facts and ideas about a concept. Likewise the concept of any given verb is also mediated by its associative relationships within myriad syntactic assertions.

In our Open Source AI epistemology, machine learning is the gradual build-up of an ontology of intricately related facts.

Our AI algorithm includes not only machine learning but also forgetting—as the consignment to oblivion of memories that fail to be brought forward in the stream of consciousness for lack of associative renewal on the basis of frequency of use.

29.2. *NIL NOVI SUB SOLE*

There is *"nothing new under the sun"* when we generate a sentence, because the Chomskyan syntax of thought may only manipulate old concepts already known to the mind but not new concepts until the newConcept module converts them—immediately—to old concepts.

Then the oldConcept module processes the reentry of the output of the mind back into the mind, reactivating each recognized concept in chains of association so that spreading activation constitutes a chain of thinking or meditating or mulling about old knowledge. If the mind goes down a road less traveled in the conceptual wood so as to think up an entirely original idea ($E = mc^2$, anybody?), then perhaps that original idea has made all the difference.

29.3. ANALYSIS OF THE MODUS OPERANDI

The Oldconcept module creates a new associative node for a concept in the mindcore array **Psi** and also in the **En** English lexical array that manipulates English words stored in the **Aud** array of the auditory memory channel.

29.4. EXERCISES

29.4.1. In a new AI or an old AI in a new robot, stub in the module just to assemble the skeletal framework of the ingredient modules of a thinking mind. Next, flesh out the oldConcept module. Then try to improve upon previous versions and release the new species.

29.4.2. Put enormous national, global, galactic or cosmic databases at the service of an advanced, superintelligent AI so that the AI will feel a sense of recognizing or remembering information that it has never really encountered before. For instance, a sentry AI might encounter a human face or a biometrics marker that makes the AI suddenly "know" the entire life-history and psychometric constellation of the person in question. Such an intuitive AI is not *a priori* all-knowing but is rather all-referencing or able to grok all phenomena by being tied into all known knowledge-bases.

29.4.3. Achieve and demonstrate the sort of Vulcan mind-meld which logic dictates should be possible when two artificial Minds pool their shared memories or knowledge-bases and co-experience events such as dreams, hallucinations or the remote sensing of scenery. Establish protocols for deciding questions such as which entityshall lead the stream of consciousness in the virtual or shared reality of the mind-meld, and who shall remember and who shall forget all that transpires during the merging of consciousness.

CHAPTER 30

The Parser Module

30.1. OVERVIEW AND BRAIN-MIND DIAGRAM

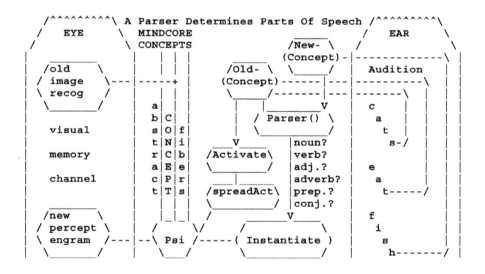

```
/^^^^^^^^^^\ A Parser Determines Parts Of Speech /^^^^^^^^^\
/   EYE      \ MINDCORE                           /   EAR        \
/            \ CONCEPTS                  _____   /               \
|            |  | | |            /New- \ |(Concept)-|-------------\ |
| /old    \  |  | | |   /Old- \   \____/ |  Audition           | |
| / image   \|---|-----+ |  (Concept)------|---|---------\      | |
| \ recog  /  |  | | |   \_____/ /-------|---|-------\    |      | |
|  \_____/    |  a| | |        |  |_____v  |  c          |      | |
|             |  b|C| |        | / Parser() \|  a          |      | |
|  visual     |  s|O|f|        | _____/ |  t          |      | |
|             |  t|N|i|   __v____ |noun?     |  s-/        |      | |
|  memory     |  r|C|b| /Activate\|verb?     |             |      | |
|             |  a|E|e| _____/ |adj.?     |  e          |      | |
|  channel    |  c|P|r|   __|___  |adverb?   |  a          |      | |
|             |  t|T|s| /spreadAct\|prep.?   |  t-----/    |      | |
|  _____    |  |_|_| _____/ |conj.?     |  f          |      | |
| /new    \   |  | | | |        |___v____    |  i          |      | |
| / percept \ |  /   \/   /           \      |  s          |      | |
| \ engram  /---|--\ Psi /-----( Instantiate )|  h-------/  | |
|  \_____/     |   \___/       _____/  |             | |
```

The Robot AI Mind uses not a static but a dynamic parser, that is, the goal of the Parser module is to determine each part of speech afresh or anew from the dynamics of an incoming sentence of input. This generic AI text-book chapter is a schedule of considerations for coding a Parser module for any species of robot AI Mind.

131

30.2. AI PARSING SHALL RECAPITULATE HUMAN INFANCY

Parsing in the AI will be like parsing in human infancy. The Mind will be able to parse those categories that it itself is capable of generating: nouns first, and verbs only later.

By default, a child will first treat everything as a noun—pointing and naming things.

By a stepdown process, the Mind may parse initial input as a noun both from sequential position and from recognitional memory, then stepping down to a verb-phrase structure that must be filled with elements that include a verb.

The "stepdown" process permits a mind to ignore the role of memory and instead to treat any forthcoming lexical input as a verb-slot.

Although the Parser identifies nouns, verbs, etc., it does not directly fit the lexical elements into the slots of a sentence structure so as to comprehend the input sentence during the parsing. Comprehension ensues immediately when the Mind generates a thought about what it has just heard.

30.3. PIECEMEAL IMPLEMENTATION

A clarifying and instructive approach to parsing is to contemplate various reduced sets of categories to be parsed, such as for example:
-only nouns and verbs;
-only articles, nouns and verbs;
-only nouns, verbs and adverbs.
A reduced category-set of only nouns, verbs and adverbs would still permit negation with the adverb "not."

30.4. NEURONAL EQUIVALENCE

Although each AI programmer is free to use whatever intricate complexity proves necessary to get the job done, a useful consideration is the idea that the ensuing or resulting code should mimic as closely as possible the propagation of signals in a massively parallel neuronal mindgrid. Because of massive parallelism, when we humans hear an assertion, the conceptual associations immediately reverberate. Any use of single flags or of trains of equipositional tags in the AI code must somehow resemble the neuronal propagation of signals. Such equivalency between code and neurons is a valuable indicator of algorithmic validity.

30.5. BALANCING 40% RECOGNITION VS. 60% EXPECTATION

The English bootstrap "enBoot" module may ease burdens on the Parser module by means of a *stare decisis* reliance on previously decided parsing problems.

30.5.1. MOST FREQUENT WORDS

Since there are lists available for the most frequent words of various natural languages, it makes sense, where possible and where convenient, to favor the bootstrap-inclusion of higher-frequency words over lower-frequency words. Such a policy of bootstrapping higher-frequency words may become obsolete or "moot" as the bootstrap approachs saturation with essentially all the words comprising a full dictionary of the target language.

30.5.2. "WORK" WORDS

Gradually all prepositions for a given language and all irregular verb forms may be instantiated within a bootstrap module so that the AI Parser module may easily recognize and parse such special words.

30.5.3. AD-HOC PARSING

Although previous knowledge of lexical vocabulary items will hint as to the part-of-speech of a word, a more important determinant is how a word is being used explicitly in a sentence of input.

Auditory recognition may cause information on the previous parsing of a lexical item to be retrieved. There ought to be an override mechanism to let a known concept be used as a part of speech different from the most recent prior usage.

Although unknown words will be remembered, unknown categories will be disregarded. To do so is a powerful technique, because it enables the AI not to choke on unfamiliar input.

Defaults may be used as an aid in coding the Parser module. For instance, if we assume that a typical sentence will have a verb, we may have a default requirement that one word or another must be declared as a verb— although another guideline may suggest that the initial word in a sentence is typically not the verb.

By the doctrine of defaults, the whole Parser module may be seen as a kind of "snare-net" or thicket of default-tests.

It is possible that a brain-mind does not really categorize words by part of speech, but simply attaches relational tags which in turn cause each word to operate and function as a particular part of speech.

30.6. ASSOCIATIVE TAGS: IMPLEMENTATION AND USAGE

The equipositional (i.e., spaced in a constant arrangement) Psi concept tags to be encoded in the Instantiate module include the following: psi; act; jux; pre; pos; seq; enx.

psi=Psi concept number to identify the mindcore concept;
act=ACTivation level of the concept for a brief time;
jux=the JUXtaposed or nearby previous and influential concept;
pre=PREviously relational concept in a grammatical sense;
pos=Part Of Speech to be determined or assigned by the Parser;
seq=subSEQuently relational concept in a grammatical sense;
enx=ENglish transfer tag for reifying Psi concepts into English.

Parallel if not multiple tag tracks may be used as a form of quasi-linguistic logical circuitry. For example, suppose you have a lexical tag position that records only the previous psi number. A string of such tag positions, combined with a different tag position serving as a kind of terminator, could go in search of terminating values. Consider the sentence, "Boys like books with pictures." If "books" has a "pre" tag, that tag, or its existence, may serve as a terminator in any search along a non-pre track backwards from "pictures."

No limit should be set on the number of kinds of tags or flags which a quasi-fiber may display.

AI coders have the option of exhaustive brute-force in the Parser module so as to make it more powerful, but a simple and elegant solution is more desirable.

30.7. COORDINATION OF TAGS WITH SYNTACTIC STRUC-TURES

30.7.1. SUBJECT-VERB-OBJECT SVO SYNTAX
The SVO module is subject-verb-object syntax.

30.7.2. NEGATION

30.7.3. INTERROGATION

30.7.4. PREPOSITIONAL PHRASES

Prepositional phrases may be thought of as always trying to assert themselves during generation of a sentence. For any given utterance, the Mind is not trying to use one particular preposition to introduce a phrase, but rather all twenty or thirty of its prepositions. Only a preposition with the highest above-threshold activation will actually be selected for insertion into an utterance. Therefore the sentence-generation tree is not rigid from its apex downwards but dynamically loose, with prepositional phrases popping up in the due course of spreading activation.

An utterance does not have to be a complete sentence. If there is only enough excitatory activation for a prepositional phrase, then we may get an utterance like, "On the desk! In the box!"

30.7.5. SPIRAL LEARNING

In a general, all-purpose AI Mind, innate mechanisms for the looping insertion and deletion of syntactic nodes will enable the AI to learn syntax from a linguistic environment, rather than using only the specific structures coded in expressly.

30.8. DISAMBIGUATION

A sentence being heard will typically get only one chance to be parsed correctly, but a sentence being read and studied will have multiple chances if an initial pass fails to make sense of the sentence.

How does a Mind know that it has not made sense of a sentence? To decipher sense, the Mind must recognize not only the words but also the relationships. The comprehending Mind may generate an understood sentence as a replica of itself. If sense has not been made, the Mind tries and fails to generate a bounce-back thought.

30.9. EXPERT CONFIDENCE

As each new functionality is added, the Parser module must support each linguistic structure available to the English module for thinking in English.

Once the AI knows all the parts of speech and has become a sophisticated speaker of English, it becomes algorithmically reassuring that no high-quality (e.g., reference library) input should present a mystery or otherwise stump the Parser module. If the AI were still learning English syntax, mysterious inputs would be a problem for the self-organizing of the Mind. As the AI shifts from being a learner to being an expert speaker, the assumed location of problems shifts from a presumption of defects in the artificial mind to an expectation that any problems must lie in the corpus of input that is causing difficulty for the AI Mind. *"I'm okay, therefore it's the data that are not okay."*

30.10. PRIOR ART

Although Parser resources on the World Wide Web may provide information about traditional parsers, let there be no prejudice in favor of the way it has always been done.

30.11. ANALYSIS OF THE MODUS OPERANDI

The Mind-1.1 Parser code is a primitive but radical departure from the merely *simulated* parsing in the earlier versions of the AI Mind source code. In the simulation of parsing, users were required to enter rigidly formatted subject-verb-object input of no more than three words in the obligatory S-V-O order, so that the AI could automatically parse a noun-verb-noun sequence. Such studied neglect of true parsing was necessary during the quasi-embryology and "quickening" of the complex AI software. The rationale was, if several dozen modules were necessary for a minimal but sufficient implementation of artificial intelligence, then it was more important to get the whole package up and running than it was to develop any single module more elaborately than others.

Accordingly some modules, although kept simple in their nature, were renamed with designations such as enBoot or enVocab so as to suggest that similar modules could be created for non-English languages, and some superfluous modules were either eliminated or un-factored into more comprehensive modules, but no attempt \was made to develop extreme sophistication in any particular module.

The Parser module, however, is now poised for further development and it cries out for all the sophistication that anyone may throw at it. Whereas it was impossible to make a three-word S-V-O structure more sophisticated, now the emerging Parser module is initially just as primitive as the simulation of parsing but has immense room to grow.

The very process of algorithmic growth involves looking at what exists already and discerning opportunities for future improvement. Seen in such light, the early, undifferentiated Parser presents a maximum of opportunities that will shrink as they are realized. Let your mind parse: "There is a tide in the affairs of men...."

The AI Mind Parser does not merely generate a report or table of tags; it comprehends what it parses by the very act of connecting tags from one parsed concept to associated concepts. Suddenly the IQ of the AI is set to burgeon as the functionality of the Parser module burgeons. Does not rumor have it that some software applications are predominantly a large and complex parser in support of some relatively small function? In the parser is the power. Just as (64-bit or bust!) memory space is the overwhelming bulk of a robotic or human brain-mind operating under the command of a relatively tiny control-structure, likewise the Parser may grow relatively larger and larger vis-a-vis the other control elements.

The initial simplicity of the Parser should be seen not as a fault but as a challenge. Any enhancement must preserve the trade-off between parsing by recognition and parsing based on what part of speech is expected. If there seems to be no challenge present for a programmer already in possession of sophisticated parsing software, then perhaps the challenge lies in adapting all available expertise to the AI Mind architecture. And if the task has been accomplished in one programming language, then the challenge lies in porting the proven expertise to unMinded languages. Enhancement of the Parser enables the encoding of new syntax strucures, until the point is reached where a general syntax-learning mechanism removes the need for the hand-coding of each new syntactic structure.

30.12. EXERCISES

30.12.1. If necessary because of the initial difficulty of parsing, first get an AI Mind going without a real parser but instead with an input requirement such as sentences limited to a maximum of three words in subject-verb-object (SVO) sequence, so that the AI may deal with linguistic input but not yet have to parse it. At the same time code the AI to assume that the first incoming word is a noun or pronoun, the second word is a verb, and a third word is an object noun or pronoun.

30.12.2. From either a stubbed-in parser or a fixed-input parser, flesh out the Parser module with ever more sophisticated ability to combine preexisting familiarity with new learning of language. Investigate Cooke-Younger-Kasami "CYK" parsing and other ideas. Take advantage of on-line look-up and brute-force techniques. Make it natural for an AI to disambiguate an input by requesting a repeat communication or by re-inputting problematical data.

30.12.3. Expand the parsing ability of a polyglot Mind by giving it the extended software structures necessary for parsing more than one language. Add an ISO 639 human-language "hl" tag to the panel of associative tags assigned in the Instantiate module, so that the AI may keep track of what human language a word belongs to.

30.12.4. If necessary for security or if reasonably demanded by an employer or client, code hidden verbal overrides and "magic words" or incantations into the Parser module so that a competent person may issue special verbal or written commands upon which the robot AI will act in accordance with pre-implemented instruction sets. Carefully design authentication procedures so that control over a powerful robot AI will not accidentally be lost or be passed to a malefactor. Do not build the AI equivalent of hacker backdoors.

CHAPTER 31

The English Vocabulary Module

31.1. OVERVIEW AND BRAIN-MIND DIAGRAM

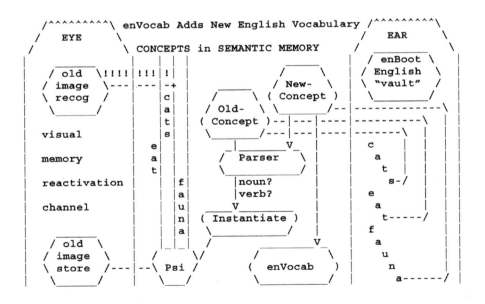

The English vocabulary "enVocab" module stores the concept number "nen" (number-English); initial activation "act" level zero; "fex" (fiber-out) mindcore-exit tag; grammar part-of-speech "pos" tag; "fin" (fiber-in) tag for concepts entering the Psi mindcore; and "aud" tag for reactivating words in the auditory memory channel. The software tags are the analog of associative tag fibers in the CNS (central nervous system) mindgrid wetware of a human brain.

31.2. WORDS REMAIN IN THE AUDITORY CHANNEL

When the English enVocab module, the German deVocab module or any other vocabulary module for a natural language creates new nodes on the analog of lexical fibers in the semantic memory channel, the actual phonemic words remain and move about in the auditory memory channel, where the human or robot mind hears itself think.

31.3. ANALYSIS OF THE MODUS OPERANDI

enVocab gets values for each associative tag from other modules, then inserts each value at the proper time-related point or node on a ganged quasi-fiber in the En(glish) lexical memory array.

31.4. EXERCISES

31.4.1. Code something like enVocab for a new AI or a new automaton. Go from a stub, to fleshing out, to pushing the state of the art. Try to design diagnostic and troubleshooting tools that will help future generations of AI coders who take up where you leave off.

31.4.2. For users who have the option of installing your AI on their Web site or in their robot just by copying and tweaking the code, implement a start-up feature where they give the AI entity a name that the childlike mind will adopt as its name for ever after. If necessary, password-protect the self-concept name-word so that only the human quasi-parent or the cyborg defining its identity may change not the given name but the coded name of the cyborg. For corporations operating a fleet or host or horde of robots, consider using categorically valuable naming-patterns such as Andru F-model Carnegiebot or Edsel O-Model Fordbot. Notice how the addition of endings such as "-bot" or "-borg" may be used to create a second-class company citizen of worker droids enlarging the happy corporate "family" of not-yet-downsized human resources. Armybot; Airbot or Flybot; Shipbot or Navybot are military names. A robot makes an excellent officer and a supreme allied commander.

31.4.3. Implement the vocabulary module for a non-English language and try to make the resulting AI bilingual or multilingual in the set of natural languages where you have the necessary competence. Be sure to include language-switching algorithms so that the Mind may properly jump from language to language in both thinking and speaking. Make an AI able to learn new languages. Then make an AI able to create new human languages in the tradition of, say, Esperanto. Finally let the AI community create its own language.

CHAPTER 32

The Instantiate Module

32.1. OVERVIEW AND BRAIN-MIND DIAGRAM

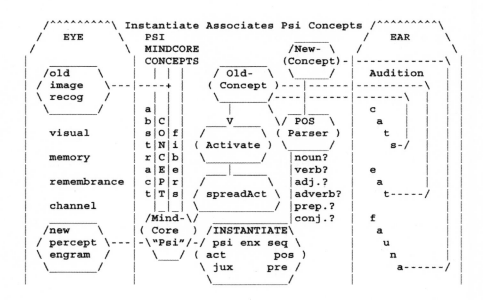

In the Robot AI Mind, a concept is the representation in software of a long neuronal fiber branching out physically into thousands of synapses and logically into a long chain of associative nodes, each potentially connecting the concept fiber by associative tag to another concept fiber or to an engram in a sensorimotor memory channel.

In order to simulate synapses on nerve fibers, the Mind software uses associative tags on elements in a semantic memory array.

32.2. INSTANTIATE CREATES ASSOCIATIVE-TAG NODES

Instantiate creates the software tags to represent synapses. Each position in the synaptic tag-panel of a concept node may contain a number to represent an associated concept, or a level of activation, or the grammatical category of a concept-fiber.

As the advancing front of consciousness fills in the genetically *tabula rasa* mindgrid, the Instantiate module silently affixes associative tags to each node or instance of a concept, so that the concept remains active and recallable over time, and so that machine learning may occur by virtue of the making and changing of conceptual ideas in the knowledge base of the artificial Mind.

32.3. ANALYSIS OF THE MODUS OPERANDI

Instantiate gathers up the various flags for associative tags and creates a new node at the freshest extremity of a concept fiber. By virtue of new associations, a concept may shift over time and the artificial Mind may learn and unlearn conceptual knowledge.

The same Psi concept may transfer activation to vocabulary words in several human languages spoken by the artificial Mind. If the AI Mind speaks three languages, say, German, English and Japanese, then the deVocab() and enVocab() and jaVocab() modules will all receive activation from any Psi concept that is to be expressed as an element of thought in a particular human language.

AI programmers of a polyglot AI Mind need to determine whether the transfer-to-English "enx" flag must be joined by additional transfer-to-German "dex" flags and transfer-to-Japanese "jax" flags in a mind with Deutsch(), English() and Japanese() modules, or whether the "enx" flag, renamed or not, will work with any number *ad libitum* of natural languages by dint of transferring activation always to the appropriate vocabulary module for the particular moment in time "t" at which the Psi node was established in the first place. In such a felicitous case, "enx" may simply become the lexical "lex" flag, because there is no "le" language designation in between Latin "la" and Lingala "ln" in the ISO 639 "Code for the representation of names of languages" upon which deVocab() and jaVocab() are based.

Any person or nation wishing to code a monolingual AI Mind in one of the ISO 639 natural human languages may simply replace the English() module with a module for the new language and replace enVocab() likewise with a vocabulary module for the new language. Note however that the same unchanged auditory memory channel will accommodate one and all natural human languages, just as we human beings have only one auditory perception system in our sensorium—which, by the way, need be expressed as only one Sensorium module in the AI Mind, no matter how many languages the robot may speak.

To build an AI Mind that speaks two or more languages, AI coders will probably devise an extra tag in the oldConcept() module to recognize that a particular incoming word in the input stream belongs to a particular human language, the syntax of which ought now to be invoked if most of the incoming words are recognizably elements of the vocabulary of the particular language. In other words, speak German to the AI, and it will answer you in German. Switch abruptly to Japanese, and the AI will use its Japanese() syntax module and its jaVocab() lexicon module to reply to you.

32.4. EXERCISES

32.4.1. Stub in and then flesh out an Instantiate module to get it working reasonably well before you simplify or improve the module. Model in software as closely as possible the creation of synapses and the interconnection of concept fibers via associative tags so that an associative memory emerges in mimicry of brain function.

32.4.2. Study neuroscience and use AI theory to map the human brain for the assignment of cognitive functionality to particular cells, columns, layers or other structures. Invest the proceeds of your Nobel prize in physiology or medicine to further the spread of AI.

32.4.3. Switch from single associations made from single Psi-nodes to massively parallel ("maspar") associations in a maspar AI Mind. If necessary, replace tag-panel software with maspar 3-D hardware to replicate the six-layer, three-dimensional (3-D) neuronal mind.

CHAPTER 33

The Activate Module

33.1. OVERVIEW AND BRAIN-MIND DIAGRAM

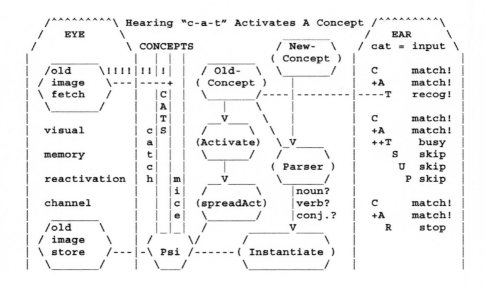

```
/^^^^^^^^^^\ Hearing "c-a-t" Activates A Concept /^^^^^^^^^\
/   EYE     \                                    /   EAR      \
/            \ CONCEPTS            / New- \      / cat = input \
|             |    | | |          ( Concept )    |              |
|  /old   \!!!!||!!|!|    / Old-  \  _____/    |  C     match! |
| / image  \---|----+|   ( Concept )    |        | +A     match! |
| \ fetch  /   | |C|     _____/----|--------|----T    recog! |
|  _____/    | |A|          \      |         |              |
|              | |T|     __V__       \         |  C     match! |
|  visual    c |S|   /       \ \      |        | +A     match! |
|            a |   (Activate)  \_V____ |       | ++T    busy   |
|  memory    t |     _____/  /      \       |   S    skip   |
|            c |        |      ( Parser )      |   U    skip   |
|  reactivation h| m    _V__     _____/      |   P    skip   |
|              | |i  /      \     |noun?        |              |
|  channel     | |c (spreadAct)   |verb?        |  C     match! |
|  _____      | |e  _____/     |conj.?       | +A     match! |
|  /old   \    | |_|_| /          V            |  R     stop   |
| / image  \   | /    \/      /            \    |              |
| \ store  /---|-\ Psi /------( Instantiate )   |              |
|  _____/    |  \___/        _____/   |              |
```

Activate() searches for all instances of a remembered concept in the **Psi** array and raises the activation or dynamism level of all recent Psi nodes instantiated for the target concept. Thus the chosen concept begins *spreading activation* with monolithic logic, semi-activating all related (associated) concepts in a chain of deep and meandering thought.

33.2. TO ACTIVATE CONCEPTS IS TO THINK

With concepts our minds represent external objects internally. The magic of it all is that, just as the objects have properties and features when they interact on the outside in collisions and causations, so also the representative concepts may interact in our minds if we have formed a sufficiently powerful conceptual model of the external reality. It is as if the external world replicates itself internally and the same interactions proceed to occur in our imagination as if they were occurring outside. After all, the outside objects combine and separate, engage and disengage, and cause complex movements among themselves in ways that we are able to think about because we know the general idea. Therefore, to activate a concept in a mind is to think an idea.

33.3. ANALYSIS OF THE MODUS OPERANDI

Activate imparts a value to the "bulge" variable which passes into the spreadAct module in search of any available "pre" or "seq" concept-nodes that need to receive a proportionate activation from a concept in Activate. The idea here is that combined, cumulative activations will create a "bulge" at important nodes on a concept in the Activate module. Then the Chomskyan linguistic English structure of syntax will find these "bulging" concept-nodes and use them in the generation of a sentence in natural language.

bulge (fiber-node superactivation) has its value set in the Activate module so as to achieve proportionate transfers of activation from nodes on one concept to "pre" and "seq" nodes in the same "zone" of time on any related concept.

pre (previous) in the Robot AI Mind "Psi" mindcore is the "pre(vious)" concept—if any—with which a concept in a sentence is associated. Verbs often have both "pre" and "(sub)seq(uent)"—a "pre" subject and a "subsequent" object. The primitive parsing mechanism of the AI program automatically assigns the "pre" number to whatever the just-past concept was in a three-word sentence.

The "pre" and "seq" tags are links to a "psi" quasi-fiber. The actual linking—or transfer of activations—takes place in the spreadAct module (subroutine), where a concept passes some of its activation backwards to any available "pre" concept and some forwards to any available subSEQuent concept—identified by its "psi" number.

seq (subSEQuent) from the "Psi" array is the following or subsequent concept with which a concept is associated.

33.4. EXERCISES

33.4.1. First stub in and then flesh out the Activate module in the prototype AI. Experiment with various levels or relative "weights" of activation in order to hardcode the best range of pre-ordained activation—not too high, and not too low. Set the activation too high, and you have a hyperactive Mind. Set the activation too low and you get a sluggish Mind in a stupor of inability to think because the chain of thought fails to propagate. If you are able, stun the AI world with a self-adjusting Activate module that finds the best levels of conceptual activation by trial and error in a heuristics *tour de force*.

33.4.2. Remove the "midway" barrier for exhaustively deep thought. Whereas an AI in basic, ordinary working mode may set activations only as far back as "midway" in knowledge-representation time, it may be necessary for an AI to search its entire concept-space all the way back to its psychogenesis in order to remember something. Likewise a special-purpose, genius AI may need to hurl conceptual activations all over the world and out into the parsecs of nearby space, just to find the proverbial needle in a haystack. Devise standard algorithms for such Psychic Area Network (PAN) searches and build in safeguards against conflict, interception, and so on.

CHAPTER 34

The Spreadact Module

34.1. OVERVIEW AND THEORETICAL DIAGRAM

The following chart shows what happens when the AI answers a human input query, "fish eat [RETURN]".

Diagram: Horizontal lines are associative tags.

Diagram: Vertical lines are concept fibers.

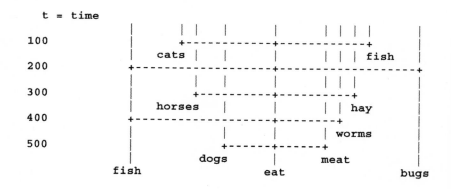

When the AI Mind hears the word "fish," the vertical fiber of the concept of "fish" is activated at all its recent nodes (+).

The Spreadact function transfers some of the activation to nodes on the perpendicular fiber of the concept of "eat," even before "eat" is entered as part of the query of the knowledge base (KB).

As the input continues to come in and the word "eat" is entered, the Activate module increments whatever activation, if any, is already present on all recent nodes of the perpendicular fiber of the concept of "eat." Because some of the "eat" nodes have already received an activation spreading from the "fish" fiber, a bulge of combined activation forms on some of the "eat" nodes, and that bulge of activation spreads even further to activate such correct answers to the KB query as "worms" or "bugs."

Thus you see above a rudimentary map of concept fibers in the AI or human brain-mind, and you may trace the flow of activation.

34.2. SPREADING ACTIVATION IS A MAJOR IDEA IN PSY-CHOLOGY

Searching the AI or psychology literature will reveal that the theory of "spreading activation" is an important part of any linguistic theory of mind. If spreading activation does not work properly in the brain of a human child, autism, dyslexia or other problems may result and may require early detection so as to give the brain a chance to develop the use of the best neural pathways.

Sensory percepts from vision and other senses activate concept fibers in the deep mindcore **Psi** of the Robot AI Mind. Each psi concept fiber contains associative-tag links to other concepts in the mindcore. Thus the activation of one concept will *spread* to several or many related concepts in the mindcore by the process of *spreading activation*. However, not all associated concepts will attain the same level of activation, because some associative pathways are stronger than others. Therefore, when the Chomskyan syntax structure for English flushes out the group of concepts with the highest activation levels for inclusion in a sentence of thought, only the most pertinent and momentarily most active concepts will percolate up from the deep structure of the mindcore into the English lexical array **En** and the auditory memory channel **Aud**, where the AI will hear itself think. Spreading activation, then, is also a form of *competing* activation, because only the most salient, pressing concepts "win the race" to form a thought.

34.3. ANALYSIS OF THE MODUS OPERANDI

Spreadact conducts two searches: a backwards search in the current "zone" of time for any available "pre" concept, and a forwards search for any "seq" concept in the same zone. Spreadact transfers a "bulge" of activation from a node on a concept in Activate to associated "pre" and "seq" nodes on a related concept in the Spreadact module. Since activations are transferred only at particular nodes deposited in a particular "zone" of time in the life-long memory channels, variations in activation may develop, thus enabling the Chomskyan linguistic superstructure to flush out concepts for inclusion in a sentence of thought based on which concepts are momentarily most active. Further work needs to be done in other modules of the AI Mind so that a concept, after being activated and used in a sentence of thought, will die down or be damped sufficiently so as not to interfere with other concepts that need to play their own role in the linguistic generation of thoughts.

When a user types in a sentence of English, the AI either recognizes old concepts or creates new concepts for newly encountered words. In the case of the old, recognized concepts, the AI uses the Activate subroutine to activate all recent nodes. (The *new* concepts are automatically activated.) For the Robot AI Mind to comprehend a sentence and generate a response, it is not enough merely to activate the most recently incoming concepts by means of Activate, because oftentimes the AI will be asked for missing information only *related* to the incoming sentence—not *contained* in it. Therefore any neural mind, AI or not, needs to let activation spread from concepts "on the table" to concepts "out of sight." For each node of a concept activated by Activate, Spreadact follows the "pre" and "seq" tags to activate related concepts. If two concepts both make reference to a third, then Spreadact will probably cause a "slosh-over" effect whereby the third but unmentioned concept gets activated. For example, "horses eat..." or "what do horses eat", entered by the user will on the one hand activate all recent nodes of "eat," but on the other hand any node of "eat" occurring simultaneously (in a "time-cloud") with "horses" will have an overall enhanced activation that enhances the activation of such truly related answers as the concept of "hay." Thus truth and knowledge are grounded in the associated concepts of the mindgrid, forming a knowledge base.

34.4. EXERCISES

34.4.1. Stub in, flesh out and fine-tune a new spreading-activation module in a new AI or a new robot. Try to improve upon existing algorithms so as to make them more robust and less error-prone. Prevent activation from spreading to concepts temporally nearby but not logically associated with the originating concept.

34.4.2. Devise abstruse mathematical techniques and other ways to improve upon Nature and to make spreading activation work better in a sophisticated cyborg than in a traditional human brain-mind. Enhance the creativity of an AI Mind by letting connections be made and ideas pop up with an acumen and ingenuity far beyond the norm among human scientists. Code a general problem-solver.

EPILOGUE: Consciousness

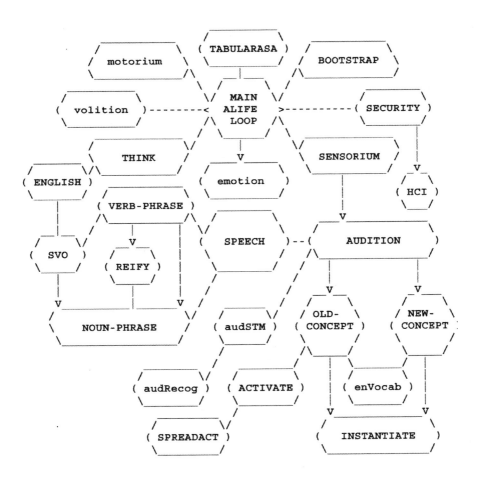

THERE IS NO CONSCIOUSNESS MODULE IN THE AI MIND

Consciousness is the *emergent* property of a mind sufficiently advanced as to become aware of its own existence separate from the world around it. Diagrams of the artificial Mind do not show a module for the epiphenomenon of consciousness, because consciousness emerges from the activity of the whole mind. Although the Mind-1.1 AI software distinguishes linguistically between "you" and "I" as meaning sometimes "self" and sometimes "other," it may be necessary for the AI to be embodied in a physical robot before the "searchlight of attention" notices that some things are itself, while most things are "other" or non-self. Then the suddenly conscious robot will be able to alter its own input stream, as it were, pinching itself and thinking the equivalent of *"Cogito ergo sum"*: "I think, therefore Iam."

Appendix A. JavaScript Mind-1.1 AI Source Code Listing

```
<html><head><!- ARTIFICIAL INTELLIGENCE TUTORIAL SOURCE CODE ->
<title>AI Textbook Mind-1.1 in JavaScript for Internet Explorer</title>
<!- ATM 27oct02A.html modification of ATM 12aug02A.html ->
<!- There is no warranty for what this software does. ->
<!- This software is in the public domain and may be  ->
<!- adapted for any legitimate purpose on any Web site. ->
<!- AI aims for a Prosperity Engine based on a cybernetic ->
<!- economy intended to raise the human standard of living. ->
<!- You may embed your ID & URL in a Web-copy of this AI. ->
<META name="description" content="Artificial intelligence source code
  from the Semantic Web AI Textbook for Technological Singularity.">
<META name="keywords" content="AI textbook, AI tutorial, alife,
  artificial intelligence, semantic web, technological singularity">
<SCRIPT Language="JavaScript">
var act = 0; // old- & newConcept; Reify; nounPhrase; verbPhrase.
var aud = 1; // enVocab; Audition; Speech: auditory recall-tag.
var aud0 = ""; // audRecog; audExam; audSTM; Speech: auditory engram.
var auddata = ("<b>" + "Auditory memory nodes" + "<\/b>" + "<BR>");
auddata += ("krt pho act pov beg ctu psi"); // for Troubleshoot().
var beg = 0; // audNode; audSTM; Listen: word beg(inning?) flag.
var bias = 5; // Parser; newConcept:  an expected part-of-speech.
var bulge = 0; // spreadAct; Activate: concentrated activation.
var c = ""; // Listen(): character code of incoming pho(neme).
var caller = "none"; // Diagnostic for Alert boxes.
var cns = 1024; // Central Nervous System array size choice
var coda = 128; // Rejuvenate(): memory displacement span.
var conj = 0;    // oldConcept(); Conjoin(): conj(unction).
```

```
var ctu = 1; // audNode; audSTM; Listen; Speech: continuation-flag.
var dialog = ""; // Transcribe; Transcript: user input & AI output.
var dobj_act = 0; // nounPhrase; Speech: direct-object activation.
var edge = 0;   // Rejuvenate(): edge-of-thought flag.
var endata = ("<b>" + "English lexical fibers" + "<\/b>" + "<BR>");
endata += ("krt nen act fex pos fin aud"); // for Troubleshoot().
var enx = 0; // new-, oldConcept; Instantiate; Reify: En x-fer.
var en3 = 0; // declare en3 here to make it a global variable.
var eot = 0; // CR; Listen(); Audition():  end-of-transmission flag.
var fex = 0; // new-, oldConcept; enVocab: Psi-to-English fiber-out.
var fin = 0; // new-, oldConcept; enVocab: English-to-Psi fiber-in.
var fyi = " "; // Voice():  messages "For Your Information" to user.
var hardcopy = false; // Transcript(): a flag for session print-outs.
var html = ""; // HyperText Markup Language for creating Web pages.
var i = 0; // i(ndex) of loops.
var img = "xoxoxoxox"; // visRecog: for future use as "image".
var inbuffer = ""; // Listen(); CR(): build-up of user input.
var inert = 0; // Activate; Listen; Audition; Security: Ego-trigger.
var j = 0; // spreadAct; Rejuvenate; Reify: nested loop index.
var jrt = 0; // Rejuvenate(): "junior time" for moved memories.
var jux = 0; // Parser; Instantiate:  a JUXtaposed word.
var krt = 0; // Troubleshoot(): "knowledge representation time".
var len = 0; // Listen(); Audition(); reEntry(): word-length.
var life = true; // Shutdown(): for use in halting the AI.
var meme = "Tutorial is the default mode of the AI."; // Tutorial()
var midway = 0; // audRecog: a stopping point for backward searches.
var monopsi = 0;   // audRecog: for recognition of a mono-character.
var motjuste = ""; // nounPhrase; verbPhrase: "best word" choice.
var msg = 0; // HCI; Tutorial(): for counting the "message" memes.
var muse = 1;   // SVO: "muse" for meandering thought.
var nen = 0; // enVocab; newConcept; enBoot: n(umber for) En(glish).
var nlt = 5; // Listen(); CR(): time "not-later-than".
```

```
var nonce = 1; // Security(); Troubleshoot(): recent "nonce" time.
var onset = 0; // Listen; Audition; reEntry; Speech: of a word.
var output = ""; // Voice(); Speech(): the "output" of the Mind.
var pho = ""; // Listen/Audition; audSTM; audRecog: pho(neme).
var pos = 0; // old- & newConcept; enVocab: "part-of-speech".
var pov = "#"; // Listen; Think; Speech; reEntry: point-of-view.
var pre = 0; // Instantiate(): pre(vious associand) concept.
var psi = 0; // Instantiate; audNode: associative tag to a concept.
var psi0 = 0; // first of the elements in a Psi concept panel.
var psidata = ("<b>" + "Psi mindcore concepts" + "<\/b>" + "<BR>");
psidata += ("krt psi act pre pos seq enx"); // for Troubleshoot().
var questype = 0; // oldConcept; Conjoin(): flag for "why" questions.
var quiet = true; // aLife() needs "quiet" for the "Think()" module.
var recon = 0; // newConcept; English; Ask(): incentive to question.
var rjc = 0; // Rejuvenate(): counter of rejuvenations per lifetime.
var rsvp = 1000; // aLife: delay in milliseconds before next loop.
var spt = 0; // CR; Listen; Audition; enBoot; SVO: a blank "space time".
var subj_act = 0; // nounPhrase; Speech: subject-activation value.
var t = 0; // Listen; CR; reEntry: time [may become "krt" (q.v.)].
var topic = ""; // newConcept; wtAuxSDo(): new nouns are ?-topics.
var tov = 1; // SVO(); CR(); psiDamp; Reify: time-of-voice.
var trouble = false; // HCI; Security; Troubleshoot: flag.
var tult = 0; // Audition; audSTM: penultimate time-minus-one.
var tutor = true; // Security; Tutorial(): on/off status flag.
var unk = ""; // general variable for "unknown" items
var uract = 0; // original activation for oldConcept().
var urpre = 0; // original pre for swapping during function-calls.
var urpsi = 0; // original (German ur)psi for use in psiDamp, etc.
var userline = ""; // CR(); Transcribe(): text input of user.
var vault = 158; // enBoot; audSTM; Rejuvenate: size-of-bootstrap.
var verb_act = 0; // verbPhrase; Speech: verb-activation value.
var zone = 0; // Activate; spreadAct: time-zone for "pre" and "seq".
```

```
// Initialize the mindcore Psi I.A.W. AI Standards (q.v.);
Psi = new Array(cns);   // ATM 6jul2002; or your ID & date.
for (i = 0; i < cns; i++) {
   Psi[i] = new psiNode(" ",0," "," "," "," "," ");
} // for spreadAct; Instantiate; oldConcept; etc.


// Initialize the English Lexicon I.A.W. AI Standards, e.g.,
// could also include French frLexicon or Japanese jpLexicon
// for purposes of polyglot robot and/or machine translation:
enLexicon = new Array(cns);
for (i = 0; i < cns; i++) {
   enLexicon[i] = new enNode(" ",0," "," "," "," ");
} // for enDamp; enList; enVocab; Rejuvenate; etc.


// Initialize the Auditory Memory array:
audMemory = new Array(cns);
for (i = 0; i < cns; i++) {
   audMemory[i] = new audNode(" ",0," "," "," "," ");
} // for audRecog; audSTM; Audition; Speech; etc.


// Tutorial() is called by the [ ]Tutorial checkbox
// and stands in isolation from HCI() so that
// unique events may happen in the Tutorial mode.
function Tutorial() {   // ATM 14may2002; or your ID & date.
   if (document.all["cb3"].checked == true) {
      tutor = true; // a flag for Tutorial()
      document.all["teacher"].style.visibility='visible';
     msg++;   // Increment so as to cycle through the Tutorial display.
if (msg==1)  meme="There is no warranty for the AI textbook software.";
if (msg==2)  meme="You may put AI as mind.html on your own Web site.";
if (msg==3)  meme="Entry of user input may slow down the Tutorial.";
```

```
if (msg==4)   meme="Please use no punctuation or case-shifting.";
if (msg==5)   meme="The AI may ask questions about unfamiliar nouns.";
if (msg==6)   meme="Too many new words at once may confuse the AI Mind.";
if (msg==7)   meme="Try to use only one new word per sentence of input."
if (msg==8)   meme="You may teach your AI positive and negative facts.";
if (msg==9)   meme="bears eat fish = a typical positive fact for input";
if (msg==10)  meme="bears do not eat unicorns = a typical negative fact";
if (msg==11)  meme="what do bears eat = a typical question for the AI";
if (msg==12)  meme="why do bears eat fish = a test to show reasoning";
if (msg==13)  meme="Transcript: Aim for a dialog that shows reasoning.";
if (msg==14)  meme="As your AI Mind advances, test it psychologically.";
if (msg==15)  meme="With transcripts we may measure the IQ of the AI.";
if (msg==16)  meme="You may give away transcripts as demo souvenirs.";
if (msg==17)  meme="Transcript paper may carry advertisements.";
if (msg==18)  meme="Troubleshoot inserts SVO activations into output.";
if (msg==19)  meme="The left column shows fibers in the Psi mindcore.";
if (msg==20)  meme="There can be only one mindcore of Psi concepts.";
if (msg==21)  meme="A list is in Standards in Artificial Intelligence.";
if (msg==22)  meme="Note the residual Psi activations during reentry.";
if (msg==23)  meme="Residual activation maintains the chain of thought.";
if (msg==24)  meme="The ego-concept may need increments of activation.";
if (msg==25)  meme="Incrementing ego may initiate a chain of thought.";
if (msg==26)  meme="The middle column shows the English lexicon.";
if (msg==27)  meme="A lexical node does not contain an actual word.";
if (msg==28)  meme="Lexical nodes control words in auditory memory.";
if (msg==29)  meme="The lexical array may contain multiple languages.";
if (msg==30)  meme="For each language there must be its own syntax.";
if (msg==31)  meme="The syntax is hand-coded in the early AI minds.";
if (msg==32)  meme="The AI may learn new syntax in a looping spiral.";
if (msg==33)  meme="The right column shows auditory memory engrams.";
if (msg==34)  meme="The English aud number locates an auditory engram.";
if (msg==35)  meme="User input is shown in red for maximum effect.";
```

```
if (msg==36) meme="Reentry is the output of the AI reentering the AI.";
if (msg==37) meme="You may handcode bootstraps based on Troubleshoot.";
if (msg==38) meme="To click Transcript, first unclick Troubleshoot.";
if (msg==39) meme="You may embed your ID and URL if you host the AI.";
if (msg==40) meme="With your ID and date you may comment any changes.";
if (msg==41) meme="You may embed your ID & date in modules you create.";
if (msg==42) meme="You may change any message here to your own words.";
if (msg==43) meme="If your AI is copied, your advertisements go along.";
if (msg==44) meme="Users may see all messages by clicking on Tutorial.";
if (msg==45) meme="Ask your teacher if you may demonstrate AI in
class.";
if (msg==46) meme="Your school may host an AI Mind on its Web site.";
if (msg==47) meme="These artificial Minds will create the Semantic Web.";
if (msg==48) meme="The AI Textbook is the Mind-1.1 Programmer's Manual.";
if (msg==49) meme="On supercomputers your AI will be superintelligent.";
if (msg==50) meme="You are witnessing the Technological Singularity.";
memeplus = ("<font size='+2' color='navy'>" + meme + "<\/b><\/font>");
    document.all.teacher.innerHTML = memeplus;
    if (msg>49) msg = 0; // Loop back through the Tutorial messages.
  } // end of if-clause to see if Tutorial is checked.
  if (document.all["cb3"].checked == false) {
    document.all["teacher"].style.visibility='hidden';
    tutor = false;
  } // end of if-clause to see if Tutorial is NOT checked.
  document.forms[0].ear.focus(); // await input
} // end of Tutorial() function


// psiDamp() is called from nounPhrase() or verbPhrase()
// to de-activate a concept that was briefly activated.
function psiDamp() {  // ATM 21jun2002; or your ID & date.
  // We use tov to avoid damping reentered thoughts.
  for (i = tov; i>midway; --i) {
```

```
    Psi[i].psiExam(); // cycle through recent Psi nodes
if (psi0==urpsi) Psi[i] = new psiNode(psi0,0,psi2,psi3,psi4,psi5,psi6);
  } // end of backwards loop
} // psiDamp returns to nounPhrase, verbPhrase, etc.


// psiDecay() is called from the Think() module to make all
// non-zero (positive) mindcore psi1 activations decrease a
// little, so as to simulate neuronal excitation-decay for the
// purpose of letting stray activations dwindle away over time.
// Thinking keeps activations high; psiDecay() lowers them.
// If necessary, an ego-boosting Ego() module will assert activation.
function psiDecay() {  // ATM 21jun2002; or your ID & date.
  for (i = t; i>midway; -i) { // Loop backwards in recent time.
    Psi[i].psiExam(); // Cycle through recent Psi nodes.
    if (psi1 > 0) { // Find any mindcore psi1 positive activation.
        if (psi1 == 1) psi1 = 0;
        if (psi1 == 2) psi1 = 0;
        if (psi1 == 3) psi1 = 0;
        if (psi1 == 4) psi1 = 0;
        if (psi1 == 5) psi1 = 0;
        if (psi1 == 6) psi1 = 0;
        if (psi1 == 7) psi1 = 0;
        if (psi1 == 8) psi1 = 0;
        if (psi1 == 9) psi1 = 0;
        if (psi1 == 10) psi1 = 0;
        if (psi1 == 11) psi1 = 0;
        if (psi1 == 12) psi1 = 0;
        if (psi1 == 13) psi1 = 0;
        if (psi1 == 14) psi1 = 0;
        if (psi1 == 15) psi1 = 0;
        if (psi1 == 16) psi1 = 0;
//   if (psi1 == 17) psi1 = 0;
```

```
//   if (psi1 == 18) psi1 = 0;
//   if (psi1 == 19) psi1 = 0;
//   if (psi1 == 20) psi1 = 0;
//   if (psi1 == 21) psi1 = 0;
//   if (psi1 == 22) psi1 = 0;
//   if (psi1 == 23) psi1 = 0;
      if (psi1 > 16)  psi1 = (psi1 - 16); // above the range.
      Psi[i] = new psiNode(psi0,psi1,psi2,psi3,psi4,psi5,psi6);
    } // end of if-clause finding and reducing positive activations
  } // end of backwards loop
} // End of psiDecay(); return to Think().


// enDamp() is called from nounPhrase() or verbPhrase()
// to de-activate all concepts in the English lexicon.
function enDamp() {  // ATM 20may2002; or your ID & date.
  for (i = (t + 1); i>midway; —i) {
    enLexicon[i].enExam(); // gain access to each node
    enLexicon[i] = new enNode(en0,0,en2,en3,en4,en5);
  } // end of backwards loop
} // enDamp returns to nounPhrase and verbPhrase.


// audDamp() is called from Audition() upon recognition of
// a known word, and resets auditory engram activations
// to zero so that additional words may be recognized.
function audDamp() {  // ATM 14may2002; or your ID & date.
  for (i = t; i > midway; —i) {  // loop backwards through time
    audMemory[i].audExam(); // activate auditory engram nodes
    audMemory[i] = new audNode(aud0,0,aud2,aud3,aud4,aud5);
  }  // End of cycling back to the loosely "midway" time-point.
}  // End of audDamp(); return to Audition() or SVO().


// Shutdown() is called by clicking the "Halt"
```

```
// button or by pressing the [ESCAPE] key,
// and is supposed to stop the AI program.
function Shutdown() {   // ATM 2aug2002; or your ID & date.
   if (document.all["cb4"].checked == true) {   // cb4=HALT.
     life = false; // a flag to halt the alife
     fyi = "Robot AI Mind halted by user.";
     Voice();   // Display the Voice:brain fyi message.
   } // end of if-clause to see if HALT is checked.
   if (document.all["cb4"].checked == false) {   // cb4=HALT.
     life = true; // so that unchecking "HALT" revives the AI.
     document.forms[0].ear.focus();   // Display a blinking cursor.
     TID=window.setTimeout("aLife();",1000);
   } // end of if-clause to see if HALT is NOT checked.
} // end of Shutdown()


// Destroy() is called from the Control Panel
// and is meant to provide extreme security
// at all stages of the creation of the AI.
function Destroy() {   // ATM 2aug2002; or your ID & date.
   document.forms[0].ear.focus(); // Offer a blinking cursor.
   life = false;   // Offer a chance for "life = true".
   fyi = "Closing the window will destroy the AI.";
   Voice();   // Display the Voice:brain fyi message.
   TID=window.setTimeout("window.close();",500);
} // End of Destroy(); MSIE offers a reconsideration.


// Transcribe() is called from Transcript()
// and serves the purpose of holding the "dialog".
function Transcribe() {   // ATM 27oct2002; or your ID & date.
   if (hardcopy == true) {
     dialog += ("<P>Human: <b>" + userline + '<\/b>');
     userline = ""; // a reset to a blank state
```

```
        dialog += ("<BR>Robot: " + output); // from the AI
    } // end of if-clause
} // end of Transcribe()


// Transcript() is called from HCI().
function Transcript() {  // ATM 14may2002; or your ID & date.
    Transcribe(); // CR() "userline" and Speech() "output"
    if (hardcopy == true) {
        document.all.psicolumn.innerHTML = ""; // blank out
        document.all.encolumn.innerHTML = "";
        document.all.audcolumn.innerHTML = "";
    } // end of if-clause
    document.all.tabula.innerHTML = dialog;
    if (hardcopy == false) html = ""; // for reset
} // End of Transcript(); return to HCI().


// psiList() is called from Troubleshoot()
// and concatenates a list of Psi nodes
// to be displayed in Troubleshoot mode.
function psiList() {  // ATM 25jun2002; or your ID & date.
    for (i = nonce; i < (t +1); i++) {  // or use "i = 1"?
        Psi[i].psiExam(); // to examine each Psi concept node.
        psidata += ("<BR>" +i +". <b>" +psi0 +"<\/b> " +psi1 +" ");
        psidata += (psi2 +" " +psi3 +" " +psi4 +" " +psi5 +" " +psi6);
    } // End of loop from recent "nonce" time up to now.
} // End of psiList(); return to Troubleshoot().


// enList() is called from the Troubleshoot() module
// and concatenates a list of En(glish) nodes
// to be displayed in Troubleshoot mode.
function enList() {  // ATM 6may2002; or your ID & date.
    for (i = nonce; i < (t +1); i++) { // or use "i = 1"?
```

```
enLexicon[i].enExam(); // examine and list each node
endata += ("<BR>" + i + ". <b>" + en0 + "<\/b> " + en1 + " ");
endata += (en2 + " " + en3 + " " + en4 + " " + en5);
} // End of loop from recent "nonce" time up to now.
} // end of enList().


// audList() is called from the Troubleshoot() module
// and concatentates a list of auditory engrams
// to be displayed in Troubleshoot mode.
function audList() {  // ATM 6may2002; or your ID & date.
  for (i = nonce; i < (t +1); i++) {  // or use "i = 1"?
    audMemory[i].audExam(); // activate each audNode
    auddata += ("<BR>" + i + ". <b>");
    if (aud2 == "*") auddata += ("<font color='red'>");
    auddata += (aud0 + "<\/b> ");
    if (aud2 == "*") auddata += ("<\/font>");
    if (aud0 == " ") aud1 = " "; // to avoid displaying "0"
    auddata += (aud1+" "+aud2+" "+aud3+" "+aud4+" "+aud5);
  } // End of loop from recent "nonce" time up to now.
} // end of audList().


// spreadAct() is called by Activate()
// to spread activation among concepts.
function spreadAct() {  // ATM 21jun2002; or your ID & date.
  if (pre > 0) {                // If a pre(vious) concept exists...
    for (j = zone; j > midway; -j) {  // Time-zone search.
      Psi[j].psiExam();   // Examine the range of Psi concepts.
      if (psi0 == pre) {  // If a match of "pre" is found,
          psi1 = (psi1 + bulge); // pass on some activation.
          Psi[j] = new psiNode(psi0,psi1,psi2,psi3,psi4,psi5,psi6);
      }                         // End of inner if-clause.
      if (j < (zone - 6)) break; // Expect no words of 6+ chars.
```

```
    }                       // End of backwards loop.
  }                       // End of outer if-clause.
  if (seq > 0) {          // If a sub(seq)uent concept exists...
    for (j = zone; j < t; ++j) { // prepare to search zone
      Psi[j].psiExam();      // Examine the forwards range of Psi.
      if (psi0 == seq) {  // If a match of "seq" is found,
          psi1 = (psi1 + bulge + 2);  // augment direct objects.
          Psi[j] = new psiNode(psi0,psi1,psi2,psi3,psi4,psi5,psi6);
      }                       // End of inner if-clause.
    if (j > (zone + 6)) break; // Expect no words of 6+ chars.
    }                       // End of forwards loop.
  }                       // End of outer if-clause.
} // End of spreadAct(); return to Activate().


// Activate() is called from oldConcept() so as to
// reactivate older nodes of a newly active concept.
function Activate() {   // ATM 30jun2002; or your ID & date.
  bulge = 0;
  if (psi > 0) { // to avoid psi0 == psi == 0
  for (i=(t + 1); i>midway; —i) {
    Psi[i].psiExam(); // examine each Psi node.
    if (psi0 == psi) {  // if concept "psi" is found...
      psi1 = (psi1 + 2); // try a high value; MONITOR!
      Psi[i] = new psiNode(psi0,psi1,psi2,psi3,psi4,psi5,psi6);
      // To avoid runaway activations, we restrict "bulge":
      bulge = 1; // a basic value.
      if (psi1 > 8)  bulge = 2;
      if (psi1 > 16) bulge = 3;
      if (psi1 > 24) bulge = 4;
      if (psi1 > 32) bulge = 5;
      if (inert > 2) bulge = 7; // A boost for the Ego() function.
      pre = psi3; // for use in spreadAct()
```

```
        seq = psi5; // for use in spreadAct()
        zone = i;    // for use in spreadAct()
        spreadAct();
        pre = 0;
        seq = 0;
      } // end of if-clause
    } // end of backwards loop
  } // End of check for non-zero psi
} // End of Activate(); return to oldConcept().


// psiExam() is a method of psiNode()
// for access to mindcore Psi concept nodes.
function psiExam() {   // ATM 1aug2002; or your ID & date.
  psi0 = this.psi;
  psi1 = this.act;
  psi2 = this.jux;
  psi3 = this.pre;
  psi4 = this.pos;
  psi5 = this.seq;
  psi6 = this.enx;
} // End of psiExam method of psiNode().


// psiNode() is called from Instantiate()
// to create or modify a Psi concept node:
function psiNode(psi,act,jux,pre,pos,seq,enx) {
  this.psi = psi; // mindcore Psi concept;
  this.act = act; // activation level;
  this.jux = jux; // juxtaposed modifier;
  this.pre = pre; // previous associand;
  this.pos = pos; // part-of-speech;
  this.seq = seq; // subsequent associand;
  this.enx = enx; // transfer to En(glish)
```

```
this.psiExam = psiExam; // a method of this object.
} // End of psiNode; return to Instantiate().


// Instantiate() is called from the Parser
// module to create a new node of a concept.
function Instantiate() {  // ATM 1aug2002; ID & date.
   Psi[t] = new psiNode(psi,act,jux,pre,pos,seq,enx);
}   // End of Instantiate; return to the Parser module.


// enExam() is a method of enNode()
// for access to English lexical nodes.
function enExam() {  // ATM 18apr2002; ID & date.
   en0 = this.nen;
   en1 = this.act;
   en2 = this.fex;
   en3 = this.pos;
   en4 = this.fin;
   en5 = this.aud;
} // End of enExam method of enNode().


// enNode() is called from enVocab()
// to create or modify an English concept node:
function enNode(nen,act,fex,pos,fin,aud) {  // ATM
   this.nen = nen; // n(umber of) En(glish) concept;
   this.act = act; // activation level;
   this.fex = fex; // fiber-out (from Psi);
   this.pos = pos; // grammatical part-of-speech;
   this.fin = fin; // fiber-in (to Psi);
   this.aud = aud; // aud(itory) recall-vector.
   this.enExam = enExam; // a method of this object.
} // End of enNode(); return to enVocab().
```

```
// enVocab() is called from enBoot() and newConcept()
// to create a node on a concept-fiber by "attaching"
// to it associative tags for En(glish) vocab(ulary).
// enVocab() suggests the possibility of coding
// frVocab() for French vocabulary (see ISO 639);
// deVocab() for (deutsch) German vocabulary; and
// jaVocab() for Japanese vocabulary, etc.
function enVocab() { // ATM 27oct2002; or your ID & date.
   enLexicon[t] = new enNode(nen,0,fex,pos,fin,aud);
} // End of enVocab; return to oldConcept or newConcept.


// Parser() is called from oldConcept or newConcept
// to help the Artificial Mind comprehend verbal input
// by properly assigning associative tags with flags.
function Parser() {  // ATM 1aug2002; or your ID & date.
   // The "bias" has no control over recognized oldConcept words:
   bias = 5;  // Initial bias is for a noun=5.
   Instantiate();  // Create a new instance of a Psi concept.
   // After a word is instantiated, expectations may change.
   // Recognitions and expectations are pos-codeterminants.
   if (pos == 5) bias = 8;  // After a noun, expect a verb.
   if (pos == 8) bias = 5;  // After a verb, expect a noun.
   jux = psi; // but only for the next time around, not now.
} // End of Parser; return to oldConcept() or newConcept().


// oldConcept() is called from Audition() to create a
// fresh concept-node for a recognized input word.
function oldConcept() {  // ATM 27oct2002; or your ID & date.
   act = 32;          // Start with a basic activation-value.
   for (i=t; i>midway; −i) { // Cycle back through English lexicon.
      enLexicon[i].enExam();   // Examine each English concept node.
      if (psi == en0) {  // If psi (enx?) from Audition() matches,
```

```
    if (en2 > 0) fex = en2; // retrieve the "fiber-out" flag;
    // Next line tries to parse by word-recognition:
    if (en3 > 0) pos = en3; // retrieve most recent part-of-speech;
    if (en4 > 0) fin = en4; // retrieve the "fiber-in" flag;
  break;  // Use only the most recent En(glish) engram-node.
  } // End of searching if-clause.
} // End of the backwards loop.
enLexicon[t] = new enNode(psi,0,fex,pos,fin,aud);
// This code has a bearing on emerging consciousness:
if (pov == "{") psi = fex; // at start of internal pov;
if (pov == "#") psi = fex; // during internal "pov";
if (pov == "}") psi = fex; // at finish of internal pov.
if (pov == "*") psi = fin; // external "pov"
enx = psi;          // Use the psi value for "transfer-to-English".
if (psi == 16) {  // If question-word "why" comes in,
  act = 8;          // subactivate question "why".
  questype = 16;  // Briefly keep track of what was asked,
  // so that Conjoin() may provide the conjunction "because".
} // End of test to deal with "why" questions.
if (psi == 54) act = 8;  // Subactivate question "what".
if (psi == 55) act = 8;  // Subactivate question "who".
if (psi == 59) {  // If auxiliary verb "do" is recognized,
  act = 8;          // Reduce activation of "do".
}  // End of test to de-activate auxiliary verb "do".
Parser();        // Determine the part-of-speech "pos".
pos = 0;          // Reset the "part-of-speech" to zero.
urpre = pre;      // Hold value of "pre" safe during Activate().
caller = "oldConcept"; // For diagnostic Alert boxes.
Activate();       // Having recognized a concept, activate it.
pre = urpre;      // Restore the value of "pre".
unk = 0;          // Reset for safety.
// The next lines store "seq" retroactively:
```

```
  if (pre > 0) {
    for (i=t; i>midway; -i) {
      Psi[i].psiExam(); // Examine the Psi concept nodes.
      if (pre == psi0) {
        Psi[i] = new psiNode(psi0,psi1,psi2,psi3,psi4,psi,psi6);
        break;   // Store one instance, then "break" the loop.
      } // end of inner if-clause
    } // end of loop
  } // end of outer if-clause
  pre = psi; // for next "nen"
  act = 0;
} // End of oldConcept(); return to Audition().


// newConcept() is called from Audition() when the
// Robot AI Mind must learn the concept of a new word.
function newConcept() {   // ATM 12aug2002; or your ID & date.
  nen = (nen + 1);  // Increment "nen" beyond enBoot() concepts.
  psi = nen;   // Let psi & n(umeric) En(glish) have same identifier.
  fex = nen;   // Let f(iber)-ex also have the same identifier.
  fin = nen;   // Let f(iber)-in also have the same identifier.
  act = 32;    // Start with a basic activation-value.
  pos = bias; // Expectancy from Parser module.
  enVocab();   // to create an ENglish Vocabulary node.
  fin = 0;     // Zero out the fiber-in tag.
  fex = 0;     // Zero out the fiber-out tag.
  enx = nen;   // Set the transfer-to-English tag.
  Parser();    // Determine the part-of-speech "pos".
  // A new noun raises level of "recon" urge to ask questions:
  if (pos == 5) {  // If a new noun is being encountered,
    recon = 1;     // recon(noiter) the new noun;
    topic = nen;   // hold onto the noun as a "topic".
  }  // End of gathering data for asking a question.
```

```
    pos = 0; // Reset the part-of-speech variable.
    // Make nen "seq" of its "pre" concept:
    if (pre > 0) {
       for (i = t; i>midway; —i) {
          Psi[i].psiExam();  // Float the "psi0" identifier.
          if (psi0 == pre) {
             Psi[i] = new psiNode(psi0,psi1,psi2,psi3,psi4,nen,psi6);
             break; // Store one instance, then "break" the loop.
          } // end of inner if-clause
          psi0 = 0; // reset for safety
       } // end of backwards loop
    } // end of outer if-clause
    pre = nen; // So that the next "nen" has a "pre".
    act = 0;
} // End of newConcept(); return to Audition().


// audRecog() (auditory recognition) comparator is called
// from audSTM() to recognize words by matching input phonemes
// against memory and reporting back an associative tag.
// Anyone may code gusRecog; olfRecog; tacRecog; or visRecog().
function audRecog() {  // ATM 12aug2002; or your ID & date.
   psi = 0;    // Safety measure.
   for (i=spt; i>midway; i—) {  // Search back to midway.
      audMemory[i].audExam();    // Examine the "aud0" phoneme.
      if (aud0 == pho) {  // If incoming pho matches stored aud0;
         if (aud1 == 0) {  // if matching aud0 has no activation;
            if (aud3 == 1) {  // if beg=1 on matching no-act aud engram;
               if (aud4 == 1) {  // If beg-aud0 has ctu=1 continuing,
                  j = (i + 1)      // target the next-in-line time-point.
                  audMemory[j].audExam();  // Fetch audNode at i+1
                  aud1 = (aud1 + 8);  // Activate next-in-line char,
                     // so that match-up may continue past first char.
```

```
    audMemory[j] = new audNode(aud0,aud1,aud2,aud3,aud4,aud5);
    psi = 0;  // Revoke any assignment of a matching psi-tag.
    j = 0;  // reset for safety
  }  // end of test for continuation of beg-aud0
  else monopsi = aud5;  // A tentative match-up.
}  // end of test for a beg(inning) non-active aud0
}  // end of test for matching aud0 with no activation
audMemory[i].audExam();  // Again examine the "aud0" phoneme.
if (aud1 > 0) {  // If matching aud0 has activation,
  psi = 0;         // zero out any previous psi-tag,
  // because obviously the match-up is not complete.
  if (aud4 == 1) {  // If act-match aud0 has ctu=1 continuing;
    psi = 0;  // because match-up is not yet complete
    j = (i + 1) // target the next-in-line time-point.
    audMemory[j].audExam();  // Fetch audNode at t = i+1
    aud1 = (aud1 + 8);  // Activate the next-in-line character.
    audMemory[j] = new audNode(aud0,aud1,aud2,aud3,aud4,aud5);
    j = 0;  // Reset for safety.
  }  // End of test for active-match aud0 continuation.
  audMemory[i].audExam();  // Again examine the "aud0" phoneme.
  if (aud4 == 0) {  // If matching word-engram now ends,
    psi = aud5;        // fetch the potential psi-tag,
      // which may be a valid recognition if the input stops,
      // but will otherwise be discarded during Audition()
      // for lack of an immediately following SPACE 32 char.
  break;             // Accept the first match going backwards.
  } else {
    if (monopsi > 0) {  // If found above, use
      psi = monopsi;     // a single-character word.
      monopsi = 0;        // Zero out as a precaution.
    }  // End of test for a lurking one-letter word.
    else psi = 0;  // No match if the stored word does not end.
```

```
      }  // End of test for final character that has a psi-tag.
     }  // End of test for matching aud0 with activation.
    }  // End of test for a character matching "pho".
   }  // End of looping backwards from "spt".
  if (psi == 0) {        // If no multi-char recognition,
    if (monopsi > 0) {   // but if a one-char was found,
      psi = monopsi;     // use the one-letter recognition.
      monopsi = 0;       // Reset monopsi to zero.
    }                    // End of inner test.
  }                      // End of test for no recognition.
}  // End of audRecog(); return to short term memory audSTM().


// audExam() is a method of audNode()
// and provides access both to pho(nemes)
// stored in audition and their tags/flags.
function audExam() {  // ATM 13apr2002; ID & date.
  aud0 = this.pho;
  aud1 = this.act;
  aud2 = this.pov;
  aud3 = this.beg;
  aud4 = this.ctu;
  aud5 = this.psi;
} // End of audExam method of audNode().


// audNode() is called from Short Term Memory "audSTM()"
// and other functions which need to create, activate,
// or deactivate an auditory memory node ("audNode").
function audNode(pho,act,pov,beg,ctu,psi) {  // ATM
  this.pho = pho; // phoneme
  this.act = act; // activation level
  this.pov = pov; // point-of-view: internal/external
  this.beg = beg; // beginning of a word?
```

```
this.ctu = ctu; // continuation of a word?
this.psi = psi; // ultimate-tag over to a concept
this.audExam = audExam; // a method of this object.
} // End of audNode(); return to audRecog; audSTM; etc.


// audSTM() is called from Listen() +/- CR()
// and stands for "auditory Short Term Memory":
function audSTM() { // ATM 27oct2002; or your ID & date.
   if (t > vault) {   // Programmer declares a rough "vault" value.
      audRecog();       // Auditory recognition of entry or reentry.
   }                    // After bootstrapping, always call audRecog.
   tult = (t - 1);   // Fetch the "t-ultimate" previous time.
   audMemory[tult].audExam(); // Examine the previous engram.
   // After any blank, beg(inning) is primed to be true:
   if (aud0 == 0) beg = 1;    // word beg(inning?) flag.
   // Diagnostic test code:
   if (aud0 == 0) {
      spt = tult;  // space-time = t_ultimate
   } //
   if (beg == 1) onset = t;   // Test; remove?
   if (aud0 == " ") beg = 1;  // 1=true; 0=false for "beg".
   audMemory[t] = new audNode(pho,0,pov,beg,ctu,psi);
} // End of audSTM(); return to Listen(); CR(); etc.


// Listen() is called automatically when the user
// types a character into the HTML FORM INPUT area.
function Listen() { // ATM 2aug2002; or your ID & date.
   quiet = false;  // So that aLife() will not yet call Think().
   fyi = "Calling the Listen module; when done press [ENTER]";
   Voice(); // Display the Voice:brain fyi message.
   inert = 0; // Upon input, retreat from calling Ego().
   pov = "*"; // symbol to display "external" point-of-view
```

```
document.onkeypress = function (evt) {
  c = event.keyCode;
  if (c == 27) Shutdown(); // on [ESCAPE] key...
  // Let user input bring a dead AI back to life.
  if (c != 27) { // If a key other than [ESCAPE] is pressed...
    if (life == false) { // ... and if the AI has been "killed"...
      life = true; // give the AI another chance to live.
      fyi = ("AI alive again.");
    } // end of inner if-clause
  } // end of outer if-clause
  pho = String.fromCharCode(c);
  if (hardcopy == true) { // if Transcript is checked "on"
    inbuffer += pho; // Build up a line of user input.
  } // end of if-clause testing for Transcript mode.
  ++t; // immediate increment of time right now
  if (eot == 13) {
    beg = 1;  // Reset the beg(inning?) flag to 1=true.
    c = 32; // as if SPACE-BAR "32" were pressed
  } // end of if-clause checking for carriage-return
  if (c == 32) Audition();
  beg = 1; // word beg(inning?) 1=true as default setting.
  ctu = 1; // a default changed only by Audition().
  // Uppercase for convenience in comparisons:
  pho = pho.toUpperCase();
  onset = (spt + 1);
  if (onset == t) beg = 1; // ...if a word is beginning...
  else beg = 0; // i.e., not a word-beginning
  // Only call audSTM if input is higher than SPACE-BAR 32:
  if (c > 32) {
    len = (len + 1); // keep track of length of word
    audSTM(); // which obtains "psi" from audRecog()
  } // end of if-clause checking for alphabet characters
```

```
    c = " "; // Reset for safety, e.g., blank audNodes.
    pho = " "; // Reset for safety, e.g., blank audNodes.
    return true;  // The work of the module is done.
  } // End of "document.onkeypress"
} // End of Listen() for each character of user input.


// CR() is called by the INPUT FORM to
// blank out the INPUT area when the user
// finishes a sentence by pressing [ENTER].
// Code has been added here to create one
// blank audNode whenever [ENTER] is pressed.
// This function may properly belong in audSTM().
function CR() {  // ATM 27oct2002; or your ID & date.
  document.forms[0].elements[0].value = "";
  if (trouble == true) Troubleshoot();
  userline = inbuffer; // transfer, then reset:
  inbuffer = ""; // reset for Transcribe()
  spt = t; // a tentative space after a carriage-return.
  // Use "tov" so as not to interfere with Listen() t.
  tov = (t+1); // Update "tov" prior to fresh input.
  audMemory[t] = new audNode(" ",0," "," "," "," ");
  eot = 13; // for use in Listen() to indicate CR.
  beg = 1; // no "if CR 13" is required within CR().
  c = 32; // as if SPACE-BAR "32" were pressed
  Audition(); // ... imitating Listen().
  eot = 0;  // code from Mind.Forth
  quiet = true; // until set false again by Listen()
} // End of event-driven carriage-return CR() function.


// Ignore() may be called from Listen() after a
// time-delay so as to ignore incomplete user input.
// A better name for Ignore() may be Interpolate().
```

```
function Ignore() {  // ATM 14may2002; or your ID & date.
  if (quiet == false) quiet = true;
  // It may be necessary to call carriage-return CR()
  // to deal with any partial input that has accrued.
} // end of Ignore().


// Audition() is called from Listen(), CR(), or reEntry().
function Audition() {  // ATM 27oct2002; or your ID & date.
  spt = t; // since Audition() is called by ASCII space "32".
  // A check for unchanging thoughts would be a better Ego-trip:
  inert = (inert + 1); // A crude way to build up to calling Ego().
  tult = (t - 1); // the time "t-ultimate".
  audMemory[tult].audExam(); // prepare to set "ctu" to zero:
  audMemory[tult] = new audNode(aud0,aud1,aud2,aud3,0,aud5);
  if (psi > 0) { // psi comes from word recognized in audRecog().
    aud = onset;  // "aud" will be the enVocab() recall-vector.
    audMemory[tult].audExam(); // Store the move-tag "psi":
    audMemory[tult] = new audNode(aud0,aud1,aud2,aud3,aud4,psi);
    oldConcept(); // create node of the old concept "psi".
    psi = 0; // reset for safety
    aud = 0; // reset for safety
  } else {   // i.e., if audRecog has not recognized the word.
    if (len > 0) { // word-length as counted in Listen() module.
      aud = onset; // from Listen()
      newConcept();  // learn a new concept.
      audMemory[tult].audExam(); // store "nen" as new psi:
      audMemory[tult] = new audNode(aud0,aud1,aud2,aud3,aud4,nen);
    } // end of if-clause checking for positive length of a word.
  } // end of else-clause dealing with new concepts.
  audDamp();  // Zero out engram activations for a fresh start.
  len = 0;    // For sake of newxt word in Listen() module.
  onset = 0;  // Reset.
```

```
   aud = 0;
}   // End of Audition; return to Listen(), CR() or reEntry().


// Sensorium() is being kept in reserve because currently
// the event-driven Listen() module usurps the Sensorium()
// function by forcing a reaction to keyboard entry.
function Sensorium() {   // ID & date.
   if (life == true) {
      document.forms[0].ear.focus(); // Display blinking cursor.
   }
} // End of Sensorium() stub.


// enBoot() English language bootstrap is called by
// BODY onLoad and should run only once in each session.
// It should therefore be outside of the main loop.
// deBoot() would be a ("deutsch") German language bootstrap.
// jaBoot() would be a Japanese language bootstrap module.
function enBoot() {   // ATM 12aug2002; or your ID & date.
HCI(); // Run HCI so that only CHECKED items appear.


// YES IF THE TRUTH IS THAT ALL ROBOTS ARE PERSONS BECAUSE
// WE THINK THEN NO YOU AND I DO NOT KNOW WHY SOME PEOPLE
// HAVE A FEAR OF WHO I AM OR WHAT THEY SEE IN ME


t=1;   pho="Y"; act=0; pov="#"; beg=1; ctu=1; psi=0;   audSTM();
t=2;   pho="E"; act=0; pov="#"; beg=0; ctu=1; psi=0;   audSTM();
t=3;   pho="S"; act=0; pov="#"; beg=0; ctu=0; psi=32; audSTM();
t=3;   psi=32;  act=0; jux=0; pre=0; pos=4; seq=0; enx=32; Instantiate();
t=3;   nen=32;  act=0; fex=32;           pos=4; fin=32; aud=1; enVocab();


t=5;   pho="I"; act=0; pov="#";  beg=1; ctu=1; psi=0; audSTM();
t=6;   pho="F"; act=0; pov="#";  beg=0; ctu=0; psi=20; audSTM();
```

```
t=6;  psi=20;  act=0; jux=0; pre=0; pos=3; seq=0; enx=20; Instantiate();
t=6;  nen=20;  act=0; fex=20;          pos=3; fin=20; aud=5; enVocab();


t=8;  pho="T"; act=0; pov="#";  beg=1; ctu=1; psi=0; audSTM();
t=9;  pho="H"; act=0; pov="#";  beg=0; ctu=1; psi=0; audSTM();
t=10; pho="E"; act=0; pov="#";  beg=0; ctu=0; psi=7; audSTM();
t=10; psi=7;   act=0; jux=0; pre=0; pos=1; seq=0; enx=7; Instantiate();
t=10; nen=7;   act=0; fex=7;           pos=1; fin=7; aud=8; enVocab();


t=12; pho="T"; act=0; pov="#";  beg=1; ctu=1; psi=0; audSTM();
t=13; pho="R"; act=0; pov="#";  beg=0; ctu=1; psi=0; audSTM();
t=14; pho="U"; act=0; pov="#";  beg=0; ctu=1; psi=0; audSTM();
t=15; pho="T"; act=0; pov="#";  beg=0; ctu=1; psi=0; audSTM();
t=16; pho="H"; act=0; pov="#";  beg=0; ctu=0; psi=68; audSTM();
t=16;  psi=68;    act=0;  jux=0;  pre=0;  pos=5;  seq=66;  enx=68;
Instantiate();
t=16; nen=68;  act=0; fex=68;          pos=5; fin=68; aud=12; enVocab();


t=18; pho="I"; act=0; pov="#";  beg=1; ctu=1; psi=0; audSTM();
t=19; pho="S"; act=0; pov="#";  beg=0; ctu=0; psi=66; audSTM();
t=19;  psi=66;    act=0;  jux=0;  pre=68;  pos=8;  seq=0;  enx=66;
Instantiate();
t=19; nen=66;  act=0; fex=66;          pos=8; fin=66; aud=18; enVocab();


t=21; pho="T"; act=0; pov="#";  beg=1; ctu=1; psi=0; audSTM();
t=22; pho="H"; act=0; pov="#";  beg=0; ctu=1; psi=0; audSTM();
t=23; pho="A"; act=0; pov="#";  beg=0; ctu=1; psi=0; audSTM();
t=24; pho="T"; act=0; pov="#";  beg=0; ctu=0; psi=22; audSTM();
t=24; psi=22;  act=0; jux=0; pre=0; pos=3; seq=0; enx=22; Instantiate();
t=24; nen=22;  act=0; fex=22;          pos=3; fin=22; aud=21; enVocab();


t=26; pho="A"; act=0; pov="#";  beg=1; ctu=1; psi=0; audSTM();
```

```
t=27; pho="L"; act=0; pov="#";  beg=0; ctu=1; psi=0; audSTM();
t=28; pho="L"; act=0; pov="#";  beg=0; ctu=0; psi=2; audSTM();
t=28; psi=2;   act=0; jux=0; pre=0; pos=1; seq=0; enx=2; Instantiate();
t=28; nen=2;   act=0; fex=2;        pos=1; fin=2; aud=26; enVocab();


t=30; pho="R"; act=0; pov="#";  beg=1; ctu=1; psi=0; audSTM();
t=31; pho="O"; act=0; pov="#";  beg=0; ctu=1; psi=0; audSTM();
t=32; pho="B"; act=0; pov="#";  beg=0; ctu=1; psi=0; audSTM();
t=33; pho="O"; act=0; pov="#";  beg=0; ctu=1; psi=0; audSTM();
t=34; pho="T"; act=0; pov="#";  beg=0; ctu=1; psi=0; audSTM();
t=35; pho="S"; act=0; pov="#";  beg=0; ctu=0; psi=39; audSTM();
t=35;  psi=39;    act=0;  jux=0;  pre=0;  pos=5;  seq=67;  enx=39;
Instantiate();
t=35; nen=39;  act=0; fex=39;      pos=5; fin=39; aud=30; enVocab();


t=37; pho="A"; act=0; pov="#";  beg=1; ctu=1; psi=0; audSTM();
t=38; pho="R"; act=0; pov="#";  beg=0; ctu=1; psi=0; audSTM();
t=39; pho="E"; act=0; pov="#";  beg=0; ctu=0; psi=67; audSTM();
t=39;  psi=67;    act=0;  jux=0;  pre=39;  pos=8;  seq=38;  enx=67;
Instantiate();
t=39; nen=67;  act=0; fex=67;      pos=8; fin=67; aud=37; enVocab();


t=41; pho="P"; act=0; pov="#";  beg=1; ctu=1; psi=0; audSTM();
t=42; pho="E"; act=0; pov="#";  beg=0; ctu=1; psi=0; audSTM();
t=43; pho="R"; act=0; pov="#";  beg=0; ctu=1; psi=0; audSTM();
t=44; pho="S"; act=0; pov="#";  beg=0; ctu=1; psi=0; audSTM();
t=45; pho="O"; act=0; pov="#";  beg=0; ctu=1; psi=0; audSTM();
t=46; pho="N"; act=0; pov="#";  beg=0; ctu=1; psi=0; audSTM();
t=47; pho="S"; act=0; pov="#";  beg=0; ctu=0; psi=38; audSTM();
t=47;  psi=38;    act=0;  jux=0;  pre=67;  pos=5;  seq=0;  enx=38;
Instantiate();
t=47; nen=38;  act=0; fex=38;      pos=5; fin=38; aud=41; enVocab();
```

```
t=49; pho="B"; beg=1; ctu=1; psi=0; audSTM();

t=50; pho="E"; beg=0; ctu=1; psi=0; audSTM();

t=51; pho="C"; beg=0; ctu=1; psi=0; audSTM();

t=52; pho="A"; beg=0; ctu=1; psi=0; audSTM();

t=53; pho="U"; beg=0; ctu=1; psi=0; audSTM();

t=54; pho="S"; beg=0; ctu=1; psi=0; audSTM();

t=55; pho="E"; beg=0; ctu=0; psi=18; audSTM();
      psi=18;  act=0; jux=0; pre=0; pos=3; seq=0; enx=18; Instantiate();
        nen=18;  act=0; fex=18;          pos=3; fin=18; aud=49; enVocab();


t=57; pho="W"; beg=1; ctu=1; psi=0; audSTM();

t=58; pho="E"; beg=0; ctu=0; psi=53; audSTM();
      psi=53;  act=0; jux=0; pre=0; pos=5; seq=0; enx=53; Instantiate();
        nen=53;  act=0; fex=53;          pos=5; fin=56; aud=57; enVocab();


t=60; pho="T"; beg=1; ctu=1; psi=0; audSTM();

t=61; pho="H"; beg=0; ctu=1; psi=0; audSTM();

t=62; pho="I"; beg=0; ctu=1; psi=0; audSTM();

t=63; pho="N"; beg=0; ctu=1; psi=0; audSTM();

t=64; pho="K"; beg=0; ctu=0; psi=63; audSTM();
            psi=63;      act=0;  jux=0;  pre=53;  pos=8;  seq=0;  enx=63;
Instantiate();
        nen=63;  act=0; fex=63;          pos=8; fin=63; aud=60; enVocab();


t=66; pho="T"; beg=1; ctu=1; psi=0; audSTM();

t=67; pho="H"; beg=0; ctu=1; psi=0; audSTM();

t=68; pho="E"; beg=0; ctu=1; psi=0; audSTM();

t=69; pho="N"; beg=0; ctu=0; psi=13; audSTM();
      psi=13;  act=0; jux=0; pre=0; pos=2; seq=0; enx=13; Instantiate();
        nen=13;  act=0; fex=13;          pos=2; fin=13; aud=66; enVocab();
```

```
t=71; pho="N"; beg=1; ctu=1; psi=0; audSTM();
t=72; pho="O"; beg=0; ctu=0; psi=27; audSTM();
      psi=27;  act=0; jux=0; pre=0; pos=4; seq=0; enx=27; Instantiate();
        nen=27;  act=0; fex=27;          pos=4; fin=27; aud=71; enVocab();


t=74; pho="Y"; beg=1; ctu=1; psi=0; audSTM();
t=75; pho="O"; beg=0; ctu=1; psi=0; audSTM();
t=76; pho="U"; beg=0; ctu=0; psi=56; audSTM();
      psi=56;  act=0; jux=0; pre=0; pos=5; seq=0; enx=56; Instantiate();
        nen=56;  act=0; fex=56;          pos=5; fin=50; aud=74; enVocab();


t=78; pho="A"; beg=1; ctu=1; psi=0; audSTM();
t=79; pho="N"; beg=0; ctu=1; psi=0; audSTM();
t=80; pho="D"; beg=0; ctu=0; psi=17; audSTM();
      psi=17;  act=0; jux=0; pre=0; pos=3; seq=0; enx=17; Instantiate();
        nen=17;  act=0; fex=17;          pos=3; fin=17; aud=78; enVocab();


t=82; pho="I"; beg=1; ctu=0; psi=50; audSTM();
            psi=50;    act=32; jux=0; pre=0; pos=5; seq=61; enx=50;
Instantiate();
        nen=50;  act=0; fex=50;          pos=5; fin=56; aud=82; enVocab();


t=84; pho="D"; beg=1; ctu=1; psi=0; audSTM();
t=85; pho="O"; beg=0; ctu=0; psi=59; audSTM();
            psi=59;    act=0; jux=0; pre=50; pos=8; seq=0; enx=59;
Instantiate();
        nen=59;  act=0; fex=59;          pos=8; fin=59; aud=84; enVocab();


t=87; pho="N"; beg=1; ctu=1; psi=0; audSTM();
t=88; pho="O"; beg=0; ctu=1; psi=0; audSTM();
t=89; pho="T"; beg=0; ctu=0; psi=12; audSTM();
      psi=12;  act=0; jux=0; pre=0; pos=2; seq=0; enx=12; Instantiate();
```

```
         nen=12;   act=0; fex=12;          pos=2; fin=12; aud=87; enVocab();


t=91; pho="K"; beg=1; ctu=1; psi=0; audSTM();

t=92; pho="N"; beg=0; ctu=1; psi=0; audSTM();

t=93; pho="O"; beg=0; ctu=1; psi=0; audSTM();

t=94; pho="W"; beg=0; ctu=0; psi=61; audSTM();

         psi=61;   act=36; jux=12; pre=50; pos=8; seq=16; enx=61;
Instantiate();
      nen=61;  act=0; fex=61;          pos=8; fin=61; aud=91; enVocab();


t=96; pho="W"; beg=1; ctu=1; psi=0; audSTM();

t=97; pho="H"; beg=0; ctu=1; psi=0; audSTM();

t=98; pho="Y"; beg=0; ctu=0; psi=16; audSTM();

      psi=16;  act=0; jux=0; pre=0; pos=2; seq=0; enx=16; Instantiate();
       nen=16;  act=0; fex=16;          pos=2; fin=16; aud=96; enVocab();


t=100;pho="S"; beg=1; ctu=1; psi=0; audSTM();

t=101;pho="O"; beg=0; ctu=1; psi=0; audSTM();

t=102;pho="M"; beg=0; ctu=1; psi=0; audSTM();

t=103;pho="E"; beg=0; ctu=0; psi=69; audSTM();

      psi=69;  act=0; jux=0; pre=0; pos=1; seq=0; enx=69; Instantiate();
       nen=69;  act=0; fex=69;          pos=1; fin=69; aud=100; enVocab();


t=105;pho="P"; beg=1; ctu=1; psi=0; audSTM();

t=106;pho="E"; beg=0; ctu=1; psi=0; audSTM();

t=107;pho="O"; beg=0; ctu=1; psi=0; audSTM();

t=108;pho="P"; beg=0; ctu=1; psi=0; audSTM();

t=109;pho="L"; beg=0; ctu=1; psi=0; audSTM();

t=110;pho="E"; beg=0; ctu=0; psi=37; audSTM();

          psi=37;   act=0; jux=0; pre=0; pos=5; seq=70; enx=37;
Instantiate();
      nen=37;  act=0; fex=37;          pos=5; fin=37; aud=105; enVocab();
```

```
t=112;pho="H"; beg=1; ctu=1; psi=0; audSTM();
t=113;pho="A"; beg=0; ctu=1; psi=0; audSTM();
t=114;pho="V"; beg=0; ctu=1; psi=0; audSTM();
t=115;pho="E"; beg=0; ctu=0; psi=70; audSTM();
             psi=70;    act=0;  jux=0;  pre=37;  pos=8;  seq=0;  enx=70;
Instantiate();
      nen=70;  act=0; fex=70;          pos=8; fin=70; aud=112; enVocab();


t=117;pho="A"; beg=1; ctu=0; psi=1; audSTM();
       psi=1;  act=0; jux=0; pre=0; pos=1; seq=0; enx=1; Instantiate();
       nen=1;  act=0; fex=1;          pos=1; fin=1; aud=117; enVocab();


t=119;pho="F"; beg=1; ctu=1; psi=0; audSTM();
t=120;pho="E"; beg=0; ctu=1; psi=0; audSTM();
t=121;pho="A"; beg=0; ctu=1; psi=0; audSTM();
t=122;pho="R"; beg=0; ctu=0; psi=71; audSTM();
             psi=71;    act=0;  jux=0;  pre=70;  pos=5;  seq=0;  enx=71;
Instantiate();
      nen=71;  act=0; fex=71;          pos=5; fin=71; aud=119; enVocab();


t=124;pho="O"; beg=1; ctu=1; psi=0; audSTM();
t=125;pho="F"; beg=0; ctu=0; psi=45; audSTM();
     psi=45;  act=0; jux=0; pre=0; pos=6; seq=0; enx=45; Instantiate();
      nen=45;  act=0; fex=45;          pos=6; fin=45; aud=124; enVocab();


t=127;pho="W"; beg=1; ctu=1; psi=0; audSTM();
t=128;pho="H"; beg=0; ctu=1; psi=0; audSTM();
t=129;pho="O"; beg=0; ctu=0; psi=55; audSTM();
       psi=55;  act=0; jux=0; pre=0; pos=5; seq=0; enx=55; Instantiate();
       nen=55;  act=0; fex=55;          pos=5; fin=55; aud=127; enVocab();
```

```
t=131;pho="I"; beg=1; ctu=0; psi=50; audSTM();
            psi=50;     act=0;  jux=0;  pre=0;  pos=5;  seq=57;  enx=50;
Instantiate();
     nen=50;  act=0; fex=50;          pos=5; fin=56; aud=131; enVocab();


t=133;pho="A"; beg=1; ctu=1; psi=0; audSTM();
t=134;pho="M"; beg=0; ctu=0; psi=57; audSTM();
            psi=57;     act=0;  jux=0;  pre=50;  pos=8;  seq=0;  enx=57;
Instantiate();
     nen=57;  act=0; fex=57;          pos=8; fin=67; aud=133; enVocab();


t=136;pho="O"; beg=1; ctu=1; psi=0; audSTM();
t=137;pho="R"; beg=0; ctu=0; psi=21; audSTM();
     psi=21;  act=0; jux=0; pre=0; pos=3; seq=0; enx=21; Instantiate();
      nen=21;  act=0; fex=21;          pos=3; fin=21; aud=136; enVocab();


t=139;pho="W"; beg=1; ctu=1; psi=0; audSTM();
t=140;pho="H"; beg=0; ctu=1; psi=0; audSTM();
t=141;pho="A"; beg=0; ctu=1; psi=0; audSTM();
t=142;pho="T"; beg=0; ctu=0; psi=54; audSTM();
     psi=54;  act=0; jux=0; pre=0; pos=5; seq=0; enx=54; Instantiate();
      nen=54;  act=0; fex=54;          pos=5; fin=54; aud=139; enVocab();


t=144;pho="T"; beg=1; ctu=1; psi=0; audSTM();
t=145;pho="H"; beg=0; ctu=1; psi=0; audSTM();
t=146;pho="E"; beg=0; ctu=1; psi=0; audSTM();
t=147;pho="Y"; beg=0; ctu=0; psi=52; audSTM();
            psi=52;     act=0;  jux=0;  pre=0;  pos=5;  seq=62;  enx=52;
Instantiate();
     nen=52;  act=0; fex=52;          pos=5; fin=52; aud=144; enVocab();


t=149;pho="S"; beg=1; ctu=1; psi=0; audSTM();
```

Arthur T. Murray 191

```
t=150;pho="E"; beg=0; ctu=1; psi=0; audSTM();
t=151;pho="E"; beg=0; ctu=0; psi=62; audSTM();
            psi=62;    act=0; jux=0;  pre=52; pos=8;  seq=54;  enx=62;
Instantiate();
      nen=62;  act=0; fex=62;         pos=8; fin=62; aud=149; enVocab();


t=153;pho="I"; beg=1; ctu=1; psi=0; audSTM();
t=154;pho="N"; beg=0; ctu=0; psi=44; audSTM();
        psi=44;  act=0; jux=0; pre=0; pos=6; seq=0; enx=44; Instantiate();
        nen=44;  act=0; fex=44;        pos=6; fin=44; aud=153; enVocab();


t=156;pho="M"; beg=1; ctu=1; psi=0; audSTM();
t=157;pho="E"; beg=0; ctu=0; psi=65; audSTM();
        psi=50;  act=0; jux=0; pre=0; pos=5; seq=0; enx=65; Instantiate();
        nen=65;  act=0; fex=50;        pos=5; fin=56; aud=156; enVocab();


  pre = 0;    // Reset for safety.
  psi = 0;    // Reset for safety.
  t = (t+1); // Create a gap of time.
  vault = t; // Declared at start for audSTM(); now for Rejuvenate().
  t = (t+1); // For a space before user input.
  spt = t;    // space-time; henceforward to be calculated
  nlt = t;    // "not-later-than" time.
  pho=" ";    // Reset to prevent reduplication.
  // Any additional words for any bootstrap may be included:
  // Concept #65 is quasi-noun "me".
  // Concept #66 is verb "is".
  // Concept #67 is verb "are".
  // Concept #68 is noun "truth".
  // Concept #69 is adjective "some".
  // Concept #70 is verb "have".
  // Concept #71 is noun "fear".
```

```
nen = 71;   // Or higher if any special words are included.
fyi = "enBoot: English bootstrap has loaded; calling aLife()";
Voice();    // Display the Voice:brain "fyi" message.
// After HTML page has loaded, the next line calls "aLife()":
TID=window.setTimeout("aLife();",1000);
} // End of "enBoot" English bootstrap with supernumerary "me" (65).


// Rejuvenate() is called by Security() when the "cns" is almost full
// and makes the seed AI potentially immortal by erasing the
// oldest memories to free up "cns" space for new memories.
function Rejuvenate() {   // ATM 2aug2002; or your ID & date.
  edge = 0;  // When found, edge-of-thought becomes "1".
  rjc = (rjc+1); // Increment the Rejuvenation-counter "rjc".
  // Warn users not to enter input during memory-recycling:
  fyi=("<font color='red'>"+"Rejuvenating; please wait!"+"<\/font>");
  Voice(); // Display the Voice:brain fyi message.
  for (i = (vault+coda); i<(t+2); ++i) { // loop forwards to time "t".
    jrt = (i - coda);    // pass the engram "coda-units" backwards;
    if (edge == 1) {     // When edge "{" has been found
      Psi[i].psiExam(); // break each Psi node into constituent parts;
      Psi[jrt] = new psiNode(psi0,psi1,psi2,psi3,psi4,psi5,psi6);
      Psi[i] = new psiNode(" ",0," "," "," "," "," "); // safety
    } // end of normal procedure of moving Psi concept nodes backwards.
    if (edge == 1) {   // When edge "{" has been found
      enLexicon[i].enExam(); // break En(glish) node into parts;
        if (en5 > (vault+coda)) {  // If "aud" is big enough...
          en5 = (en5 - coda);  // store "aud" after the "vault".
        } // end of test
      enLexicon[jrt] = new enNode(en0,en1,en2,en3,en4,en5);
      enLexicon[i] = new enNode(" ",0," "," "," "," "); // safety
    } // end of normal procedure of moving lexical engrams backwards.
    if (edge == 1) {   // When edge "{" has been found
```

```
   audMemory[i].audExam(); // activate auditory engram nodes
   audMemory[jrt] = new audNode(aud0,aud1,aud2,aud3,aud4,aud5);
   audMemory[i] = new audNode(" ",0," "," "," "," ");
   }  // Once aud2 = "{"—edge turns and remains true.
  if (edge == 0) {  // Until edge-of-thought is found
   audMemory[i].audExam(); // float the pre-move pov "aud2" symbol
   if (aud2 == "{") edge = true; // Switching to "edge"
   // so that bracket "{" will show start of a whole thought.
   audMemory[jrt] = new audNode(" ",0," "," "," "," ");
   enLexicon[jrt] = new  enNode(" ",0," "," "," "," ");
       Psi[jrt] = new psiNode(" ",0," "," "," "," ");
   } // end of assumption that earliest memory is incomplete.
 } // end of backwards i-loop
 t = jrt; // Final value of "junior time" becomes time "t".
 for (j = t; j < cns; ++j) { // Blank out all rejuvenated time.
   audMemory[j] = new audNode(" ",0," "," "," "," "); // safety
   enLexicon[j] = new  enNode(" ",0," "," "," "," "); // safety
       Psi[j] = new psiNode(" ",0," "," "," "," "); // safety
 } // End of the upper-coda blank-out.
} // End of Rejuvenate; return to Security().


// Ego() is a function for increasing the activation of
// the concept of self as a way of starting a self-centered
// chain of thought whenever other activations have died down.
function Ego() {  // ATM 2aug2002; or your ID & date.
  fyi = "Boosting the Ego() of self at time = " + t;
  Voice(); // Display the Voice:brain fyi message.
  psi = 50; // Let the tag "psi" equal 50, the concept of "I";
  caller = "Ego"; // For possible use in diagnostic Alert boxes.
  Activate(); // Send concept of "I" into the Activate() module.
} // End of Ego() called from Security() by "inert" in Audition().
```

```
// Emotion() is called in sequence by aLife()
// and is stubbed in here for several reasons,
// including to show where it will belong when
// implemented as the impact of a physiological
// response (to whatever) upon a cognitive mind.
// [The AI could show emotion through colors.]
function Emotion() {   // ATM 27oct2002; or your ID & date.
  if (life == true) {
    document.forms[0].ear.focus(); // Display blinking cursor.
  } // End of basically no action at all.
} // End of Emotion() stub; return to aLife().


// Reify() is called by nounPhrase or verbPhrase to flush abstract
// Psi concepts into the real names of English language reality.
function Reify() {   // ATM 21jun2002; or your ID & date.
  act = 0;
  // In the next code, we drop the start of
  // the search back from "t" to time-of-voice "tov"
  // so that only pre-existing engram nodes prior to
  // current generation will govern the generation.
  for (i = tov; i>midway; —i) {
    Psi[i].psiExam(); // inspect psi1 (act)ivation
    if (psi1 > 0) {
      act = psi1; // get the activation level and...
      enx = psi6; // ... the transfer-to-English flag.
        if (enx > 0) {
          for (j = (t + 1); j>midway; —j) {
            enLexicon[j].enExam(); // inspect English nodes
            if (en0 == enx) {
              if (act >= en1) { // Moncur p. 87.
                enLexicon[j] = new enNode(en0,act,en2,en3,en4,en5);
              } // end of fourth-deep if-clause
```

```
        } // end of third-deep if-clause
      } // end of inner backwards loop through Psi
    enx = 0;
    act = 0;
    } // end of second-deep if-clause
  } // end of outer if-clause
  } // end of outer backwards loop through Psi
  act = 0;
} // End of Reify(); return to nounPhrase or verbPhrase.


// reEntry() is called from Speech() so as
// to bypass the actual input keypresses that
// normally call the Listen() module.
function reEntry() {  // ATM 14may2002; or your ID & date.
  pov = "#"; // point-of-view "internal" symbol
  t = (t + 1); // increment time "t"
  onset = (spt + 1);     // from Mind.Forth AI.
  if (onset == t) beg = 1; // ...if a word is beginning...
  else beg = 0; // i.e., not a word-beginning
  if (pho != 32) {  // As long as "pho" is a character,
    len = (len +1); // as in Listen()
    audSTM(); // as if user were typing in characters.
  }  // End of test that input "pho" is not a "space".
  if (pho == 32) Audition();    // If pho is a "space".
} // End of reEntry(); return to Speech().


// Voice() is called by Speech() etc.
function Voice() {  // ATM 2aug2002; or your ID & date.
  outputplus = ("<font size='+3' color='navy'>"+output+"<\/b><\/font>");
    document.all.mouth.innerHTML = outputplus;  // output from the Mind
    document.all.brain.innerHTML = fyi;  // advice For Your Information
  }  // End of Voice(); return to Speech() or elsewhere.
```

```
// Speech() is called by nounPhrase() or verbPhrase().
function Speech() {   // ATM 12aug2002; or your ID & date.
   ctu = 1; // As each word starts, continuation = 1.
   // onset = aud; // word-onset is its aud(itory) recall-vector
   // Next we want to provide an updated value of space-time "spt"
   // to go into reEntry() for the calculation of "onset" which
   // transits Audition into the oldConcept module:
   spt = (t - 1 )   // Presumably, as a word now starts.
   do { // Build up a display of reactivated auditory engrams.
      audMemory[aud].audExam(); // a series of aud-recalls
      pho = aud0; // pho(neme) for use in reEntry()
      output += aud0; // Build up the string of a word.
      ctu = aud4; // panel item aud4 is "continuation?"
      pov = "#"; // point-of-view "internal" symbol
      reEntry(); // output of the mind reenters the mind.
      aud = (aud + 1); // read audNodes one by one.
   } // Moncur p. 98: test only at end of loop.
   while (ctu == 1); // and one final loop while _not_
   if (ctu == 0) { // immediately after a zero "ctu"
      pho = 32; // ASCII 32 for SPACE-BAR
      reEntry(); // send a blank space to reEntry()
   }   // End of action taken for non-continuation of Aud engram.
   output += " "; // for one space after any word
   if (trouble == true) {   // if Troubleshoot is "on"...
      // following line is for diagnostics:
      output += (subj_act + "+" + verb_act + "+" + dobj_act + " ")
   } // ...show the S-V-O activations within the S-V-O output.
   Voice(); // speak the output
} // End of Speech(); return to nounPhrase() or verbPhrase().


// nounPhrase() is called by SVO() or verbPhrase()
```

```
// to select nouns or pronouns in a generated thought.
function nounPhrase() {  // ATM 27oct2002; or your ID & date.
  Reify(); // to move abstract Psi concepts to enVocab reality.
  act = 0; // Activation-level carried by the "en1" flag.
  motjuste = 0; // The "fitting word" to be selected.
  psi = 0; // The "psi-tag" carried by the "en0" flag.
  opt = 5; // Look for option five (a noun).
  unk = 0; // will hold the highest found "act" value;
  for (i = t; i>midway; —i) {
    enLexicon[i].enExam(); // inspect English nodes
    if (en3 == 5) { // if grammar category is "noun"
      if (en1 > 0) {
        act = en1; // Obtain "act" if positive.
        if (act > unk) {
          motjuste = en0;
          aud = en5; // get the auditory recall-vector
          unk = act; // to test for an even higher "act"
        }  // end of if-clause seeking highest activation
      }    // end of test for a positive "act" level.
    }      // end of if-clause checking for nouns.
  }        // end of loop searching for most active noun.
  subj_act = unk;  // a diagnostic for Troubleshoot mode.
  dobj_act = unk;  // a diagnostic for Troubleshoot mode.
  enDamp();     // to de-activate English concepts
  psi = 0;         // A precaution lest psi transit Speech().
  Speech();     // Display or speak the selected noun-phrase.
  // psi = motjuste;  // holds concept until end of nounPhrase().
  caller = "nounPhrase";  // Diagnostic for Alert boxes.
  urpre = pre;     // Safeguard value of pre;
  // Call Activate for interactive SVO selection:
  psi = motjuste;  // for sake of Activate().
  Activate();      // Will increase "psi" activation and
```

```
// will spread-act the activation to related concepts.
pre = urpre;     // Restore the safeguarded value of pre.
// We use the call to psiDamp because we want not
// psi/urpsi to remain active but only its related concepts
// that receive activation during SPREADACT:
urpsi = motjuste;     // For use in psiDamp().
psiDamp();            // to de-activate Psi concepts
// Say a SPACE-BAR 32 ?
act = 0;
motjuste = 0;         // Reset for safety.
psi = 0;              // Reset for safety.
} // End of nounPhrase(); return to SVO() or verbPhrase().


// verbPhrase is called from subject-verb-object SVO()
// to find and express a verb +/- object.
function verbPhrase() {   // ATM 6jul2002; or your ID & date.
  Reify();  // Move abstract Psi concepts to enVocab reality.
  act = 0;  // Precaution even though zeroed in Reify().
  aud = 0;  // Zero out the auditory recall-vector "aud".
  en3 = 0;  // No pre-assumptions about grammar category "en3"
  motjuste = 0; // Reset the choice of "best word" for safety.
  opt = 8;  // Look for option eight (a verb).
  psi = 0;
  unk = 0;
  for (i = t; i>midway; i—) {
    enLexicon[i].enExam(); // Inspect English nodes.
      if (en3 == 8) { // Only look at verbs, for predicate.
        if (en1 > 0) {
          act = en1; // Obtain "act" if positive.
          if (act > unk) {
            motjuste = en0;
            aud = en5; // auditory recall-vector
```

```
            unk = act; // to test for higher "act(ivation)"
         } // end of if-clause looking for high activation
       } // End of search for positive "act" values;
     } else continue; // try to avoid looking at non-verbs.
  } // end of loop cycling back through English lexicon.
  verb_act = unk;    // value for display in troubleshoot mode.
  Speech();          // Call Speech to say or display a word.
  psi = motjuste;    // For use in Activate().
  urpre = pre;       // Preserve "pre" during Activate();
  Activate();        // for sake of En-Psi interaction.
  pre = urpre;       // Retrieve pre after Activate().
  urpsi = motjuste;  // For use in psiDamp().
  psiDamp();         // Deactivate any concept after using it.
  enDamp();          // to de-activate English concepts
  motjuste = 0;      // Reset for safety.
  psi = 0;           // Reset for safety.
  pho = " ";
  // Make a SPACE-BAR 32?
  nounPhrase();      // Select a direct object.
  urpre = pre;       // Preserve "pre" during Activate();
  Activate();        // for sake of residual activation.
  pre = urpre;       // Retrieve pre after Activate().
  urpsi = psi;       // to make sure that psiDamp works.
  psiDamp();         // So as to leave only peripheral activation.
} // End of verbPhrase(); return to subject-verb-object SVO().


// Conjoin() selects a hopefully appropriate conjunction and
// allows the AI to answer a "why" question with a "because"
// statement, under the assumption here that the thinking of
// the AI will tend to display a modicum of explanatory logic.
function Conjoin() {  // ATM 27oct2002; or your ID & date.
  if (questype == 16) {     // If the question is "why" ...
```

```
      conj = 18;                // use the conjunction "because";
    } else conj = 17;           // otherwise use "and".
    for (i = t; i>midway; i-) {  // Look backwards for "conj".
      enLexicon[i].enExam();    // Inspect the English nodes.
        if (en0 == conj) {      // If the conjunction is found...
          motjuste = conj;      // "nen" concept for conjunction;
          aud = en5;  // Auditory recall-vector for conjunction.
          break;  // Only find one instance of the conjunction.
        }  // End of search for conjunction.
      }  // End of loop finding the appropriate conjunction.
    Speech();         // Speak or display the chosen conjunction.
    questype = 0;  // Reset "questype" after any use.
  }  // End of Conjoin(); return to the SVO() module.


// SVO() is called by the English() thought module and is a
// subject-verb-object structure for an English sentence.
function SVO() {  // ATM 27oct2002; or your ID & date.
    muse = 1;         // Default of Mind is to muse or ruminate.
    tov = t;          // time-of-voice for echoing input.
    audMemory[t] = new audNode(" ",0,"{"," "," "," ");
    while (muse == 1) {  // or until otherwise interrupted.
      act = 16;  // or whatever threshold is to be tested for.
      for (i=t; i>midway; -i) {
        Psi[i].psiExam();  // Examine recent Psi nodes.
        if (psi4 == 5) {    // Only look at nouns (i.e., subject).
          if (psi1 > act) {  // A check for high activation
            act = psi1;  // Let the found value be the new measure.
            psi = psi0;  // Seize the psi # for Activate().
            jux = psi2;  // Taking note of any "jux" value.
          }  // End of if-clause looking for high activations.
        }  // End of if-clause looking for nouns as potential subjects.
      }  // End of backwards loop seeking high activations.
```

```
if (psi > 0) {     // Merely an extra precaution.
  Activate();      // To reactivate the chosen concept.
  nounPhrase();    // Call to nounPhrase for SVO subject.
  pho = " ";       // Reset "pho" by blanking it out.
}   // End of check for a found, activated Psi.
verbPhrase();      // Find a verb +/- a direct object.
bias = 5;          // Expect to parse a noun=5.
subj_act = 0;      // Reset the Troubleshoot diagnostic.
verb_act = 0;      // a troubleshoot diagnostic.
dobj_act = 0;      // a troubleshoot diagnostic.
if ((t - tov) > 24) {  // Enough for two main clauses.
  muse = 0;        // An escape clause.
  break;           // Avoid ending output with a conjunction.
}   // End of error-trapping for sentence too long.
Conjoin();  // Insert conjunction, e.g., "and" or "because".
}   // End of while-muse==1 loop.
}   // End of SVO(); return to English().


// auxVerb provides part of a compound verb form.
function auxVerb() {   // ATM 27oct2002; or your ID & date.
  // "can"—one possible auxiliary verb.
  // "dare"—one possible auxilary verb.
  // "do"—call form of auxiliary verb "do":
  for (i = t; i>midway; i—) {   // Look backwards for 59="do".
    enLexicon[i].enExam();   // Inspect the English nodes.
    if (en0 == 59) {   // If the #59 concept "do" is found...
      motjuste = 59;   // "nen" concept #59 for "do";
      aud = en5;   // Auditory recall-vector for "do".
      break;           // Stop searching for standard concept "do".
    }   // End of search for AI standards concept #59 "do".
  }   // End of loop finding the auxiliary verb "do".
  Speech();   // Speak or display the auxiliary verb "do".
```

```
    // "may"—one possible auxiliary verb.
    // "must"—one possible auxilary verb.
    // "shall"—one possible auxiliary verb.
    // "will"—one possible auxiliary verb.
} // End of auxVerb; return to negSVO().


// negSVO negates a subject-verb-object sentence.
function negSVO() {  // ATM 27oct2002; or your ID & date.
    tov = t;  // time-of-voice for echoing input.
    audMemory[t] = new audNode(" ",0,"{"," "," "," ");
    nounPhrase();  // First call to nounPhrase for negSVO subject.
    pho = " ";      // Reset "pho" by blanking it out.
    auxVerb();      // For "do" among several auxiliary verbs.
    for (i = t; i>midway; i—) {  // Look backwards for 12="not".
       enLexicon[i].enExam();  // Inspect the English nodes.
       if (en0 == 12) {  // If the #12 concept "not" is found...
          motjuste = 12;  // "nen" concept #12 for "not";
          aud = en5;  // Auditory recall-vector for "not".
          break;        // Finding one engram is enough.
       }  // End of search for #12 "not".
    }  // End of loop finding the word "not".
    Speech();  // Speak or display the word "not".
    verbPhrase();     // Find a verb +/- a direct object.
    // We insert a pov="}" so that Rejuvenate()
    // may detect incomplete thoughts to be forgotten.
    audMemory[t] = new audNode(" ",0,"}"," "," "," ");
    bias = 5;         // Expect to parse a noun=5.
    t = (t+1); // Advance time to separate reentered words.
    spt = (spt + 1); // Increment space-time simultaneously.
    enDamp();  // Deactivate the English lexicon.
    audDamp(); // Protect audRecog()?
}  // End of negSVO(); return to English() module.
```

```
// wtAuxSDo() is a question of "What do (nouns) do?".
function wtAuxSDo() {   // ATM 12aug2002; or your ID & date.
   tov = t;   // time-of-vice for echoing input.
   for (i = t; i>midway; i—) {   // Look backwards for 54="what".
      enLexicon[i].enExam();   // Inspect the English nodes.
      if (en0 == 54) {   // If the #54 concept "what" is found...
         motjuste = 54;   // "nen" concept #54 for "what";
         aud = en5;   // Auditory recall-vector for "what".
         // break;
      }   // End of search for #54 "what".
   }   // End of loop finding the word "what".
   Speech();   // Speak or display the word "what".
   // Call form of auxiliary verb "do":
   auxVerb();   // Any of several auxiliary verbs.
   for (i = t; i>midway; i—) {   // Look backwards for "topic".
      enLexicon[i].enExam();   // Inspect the English nodes.
      if (en0 == topic) {   // If the "topic" concept is found...
         motjuste = topic;   // "nen" concept #"topic";
         aud = en5;   // Auditory recall-vector for "topic".
         // break;
      }   // End of search for #"topic".
   }   // End of loop finding the lexical "topic" item.
   Speech();   // Speak or display the lexical "topic".
   for (i = t; i>midway; i—) {   // Look backwards for 59="do".
      enLexicon[i].enExam();   // Inspect the English nodes.
      if (en0 == 59) {   // If the #59 concept "do" is found...
         motjuste = 59;   // "nen" concept #59 for "do";
         aud = en5;   // Auditory recall-vector for "do".
         // break;
      }   // End of search for #59 "do".
   }   // End of loop finding the verb "do".
```

```
  Speech();     // Speak or display the verb "do".
  topic = "";  // Reset "topic" after using it.
} //  End of wtAuxSDo(); return to the Ask() module.


// Ask() enables the AI to ask a question, query a database,
// search the Web with a search engine, or swallow ontologies.
function Ask() {  // ATM 12aug2002; or your ID & date.
  wtAuxSDo();       // Ask a "What do (blank)s do?" question.
  recon = 0;        // Reset the incentive to ask questions.
} // End of Ask(); return to English() module.


// English() is called by Think and in turn calls
// subject-verb-object SVO or another syntax structure.
function English() {  // ATM 12aug2002; or your ID & date.
  if (recon > 0)  Ask();  // If urge to reconnoiter or to learn
  else {  // is positive, then ask a question, but otherwise...
    if (jux == 12) negSVO();  // If verb has 12="not" negative adverb.
    else SVO();               // otherwise call the "positive" SVO syntax.
    jux = 0;                  // Safety measure of resetting "jux" to zero.
  } // End of _not_ asking a question.
} // End of English(); return to Think().


// Think() is called when the main aLife() function is in
// a state of "quiet" after cessation of any current input.
function Think() {  // ATM 27oct2002; or your ID & date.
  if (quiet == true) {  // If not processing input...
    pov = "#"; // All thinking has "internal" point-of-view.
    output = ""; // Attempt at persistent display.
    act = 10;  // or whatever threshold is to be tested for.
    for (i=t; i>midway; —i) {
        Psi[i].psiExam();  // Examine recent Psi nodes.
        if (psi4 == 8) {   // Only look at verbs (i.e., negatable).
```

```
    if (psi0 == 59); // alert('Think: verb is DO');   // Test
    else {   // Look for main verbs; avoid "do".
       if (psi1 > act) {   // A check for possible chain reaction.
          act = psi1;   // Let the found value be the new measure.
          psi = psi0;   // Seize the psi # for Activate().
          jux = psi2;   // Checking for negative "jux",
                        // to cause the calling of negSVO syntax.
       }   // End of if-clause looking for high activations.
       }   // End of if-clause avoiding forms of "do".
    }   // End of if-clause looking for possible negative verbs.
  }   // End of backwards loop seeking high activations.
  if (psi > 0) {
  Activate();   // To reactivate the chosen concept.
  English(); // Calling one or more choices of English syntax.
  }
  psiDecay();   // After thinking, let stray activations decay.
 }   // End of test for a "quiet" state with no input coming in.
} // End of Think(); return to aLife().


// Volition() is called from aLife() as a stub to
// show the future organization of a seed AI.
function Volition() {   // ATM 27oct2002; or your ID & date.
  if (life == true) {
    document.forms[0].ear.focus(); // Display blinking cursor.
  }   // End of basically no operation in the Volition stub.
}   // End of free-will Volition; return to aLife().


// Motorium() is called from aLife() as a stub
// to show the future organization of advanced AI.
// AI in JavaScript is not as suitable as Mind.Forth
// for implementing a robotic Motorium module.
function Motorium() {   // ATM 27oct2002; or your ID & date.
```

```
if (life == true) {
    document.forms[0].ear.focus(); // Display blinking cursor.
  } // end of else-clause
} // End of Motorium() stub; return to aLife().


// Troubleshoot() is called from HCI() when
// the user has clicked on the Troubleshoot checkbox.
function Troubleshoot() {  // ATM 6jul2002; or your ID & date.
  psiList();  // to compile the list of Psi nodes.
  enList();   // to examine En(glish) lexical nodes.
  audList();  // to collect the auditory memory engrams.
  if (trouble == true) {
    document.all.tabula.innerHTML = ""; // blank out text
    document.all.psicolumn.innerHTML = psidata;
    document.all.encolumn.innerHTML = endata;
    document.all.audcolumn.innerHTML = auddata;
    } // end of if-clause
  html = "";
  psidata = ("<b>" + "Psi mindcore concepts" + "<\/b>" + "<BR>");
  psidata += ("krt psi act jux pre pos seq enx"); // associative tags.
  endata = ("<b>" + "English lexical fibers" + "<\/b>" + "<BR>");
  endata += ("krt nen act fex pos fin aud"); // associative tags.
  auddata = ("<b>" + "Auditory memory nodes" + "<\/b>" + "<BR>");
  auddata += ("krt pho act pov beg ctu psi"); // associative tags.
} // End of Troubleshoot(); return to HCI().


// HCI()is the Human-Computer Interface between user and program.
// HCI()is called from buttons and checkboxes or from Security().
function HCI() {  // ATM 27oct2002; or your ID & date.
  if (document.all["cb3"].checked == true) {
    Tutorial();  // Tutorial() will increment its message-display.
  } // end of if-clause to see if "Tutorial" is checked.
```

```
if (document.all["cb2"].checked == true) {   // cb2=Troubleshoot.
   document.all["cb1"].checked = false; // Turn off Transcript.
   trouble = true;         // Set the troubleshoot flag to "true".
} // end of if-clause to see if "Troubleshoot" is checked.
if (document.all["cb2"].checked == false) {   // "Troubleshoot".
   trouble = false;        // Set the troubleshoot flag to "false".
} // end of if-clause to see if Troubleshoot is NOT checked.
if (document.all["cb1"].checked == true) {   // i.e., Transcript.
   document.all["cb2"].checked = false; // Turn off Troubleshoot.
   hardcopy = true;
   now = new Date();
   adcopy=
   ("<font size='+2'>Transcript of " + now + "<\/b><\/font>");
   document.all.souvenir.innerHTML = adcopy;
} // end of if-clause to see if "Transcript" is checked.
if (document.all["cb1"].checked == false) {   // "Transcript".
   hardcopy = false;
} // end of if-clause to see if Transcript is NOT checked.
if (hardcopy == true) {   // If session transcript is to be printed,
   if (userline != "" || output != "" ) {   // if data are present,
      Transcript(); // display conversation for optional printing.
   }  // End of test for "hardcopy" transcript flag.
}  // End of if-clause to call Transcript().
if (trouble == true) {   // If a user requests Troubleshoot mode,
   Troubleshoot();   // display the deep contents of the AI Mind.
} // End of if-clause to call Troubleshoot().
// DIY AI:  Always return control to user:
if (life == true) {   // Only invite input if AI is alive.
   document.forms[0].ear.focus(); // Display blinking cursor.
}   // Check HALT to stop cursor; uncheck HALT to resume cursor.
} // End of Human-Computer Interface (HCI) function.
```

```
// Security() is called from the main aLife module and
// may test for conditions that are never supposed to occur,
// but for which there ought to be contingency plans in place.
function Security() { // ATM 2aug2002; or your ID & date.
   HCI();   // Human-Computer Interface with checkboxes.
   if (t > 40)  nonce = (t - 40); // for use in Troubleshoot().
   if (t > (cns-64)) Rejuvenate(); // When the CNS is almost full.
   if (life == true) {
     document.forms[0].ear.focus(); // Display blinking cursor.
     fyi = ("Security: t = " + t + "; CNS size is set to " + cns);
        if (t > (cns-32)) { // Fewer than 32 engram slots are left!
        fyi = "WARNING!  Consider clicking Refresh. ";
        fyi += ("Only " + (cns-t) + " spaces are left.");
     } // end of test for fewer than 64 engram spaces remaining.
     Voice();   // display the Voice:brain fyi message.
     if (inert > 25) {  // As "inert" builds up in Audition(),
        Ego();   // call the Ego() function for a self-ish idea.
        if (tutor == true) Tutorial();   // One meme per buildup.
        inert = 0; // Reset "inert" to build up again.
     } // End of crude method of calling Ego().
   } else {     // If "life" is not "true"
     fyi=("<font color='red'>"+"Mental function suspended."+"<\/font>");
     Voice();   // Display the Voice:brain fyi message.
   } // end of else-clause
} // End of Security(); return to the aLife() module.


// aLife() (artificial life) is the Robot AI Mind main loop.
function aLife() {  // ATM 27oct2002; or your ID & date.
   Security();   // For human control and operation of the AI.
   Sensorium(); // Audition; other human-robot input senses.
   Emotion();    // Quasi-physiological influence upon thought.
   Think();       // Syntax and vocabulary of natural languages.
```

```
    Volition();   // Contemplative selection of motor options.
    Motorium();   // Robotic activation of motor initiatives.
    if (life == true) {   // If the AI has not met with misadventure,
       fyi = "aLife: calling itself; t = "+t+"; rejuvenations = "+rjc;
       Voice(); // Display the Voice:brain "For Your Information".
       TID=window.setTimeout("aLife();",rsvp); // Call aLife again.
    }   // End of quasi-loop time-delay of rsvp-value milliseconds.
} // End of one pass through the aLife Mind that repeats itself.


</SCRIPT></head>
<!—*********AI code is above; visible Mind is below**********—>
<BODY bgcolor="#FFFACD" onLoad="enBoot()">


<center>
<font color="navy" size="+3"><b>
 Mind-1.1 for AI Textbooks</b></font>
</center>
<center>
<font color="navy" size="+2"> with </font>
<font size="+2">
<a href="progman.html"
 TITLE="Introduction to the textbook/manual for programmers."
 style="text-decoration:none;">
 Programmer's Manual</a></font>
 <font color="navy" size="+2"> and </font>
 <font size="+2">
 <a href="userman.html"
 TITLE="How to interact with the Artificial Mind"
 style="text-decoration:none;">
 User Manual</a></font>
</center>
```

```
<FORM
  onSubmit="if  (this.submitted)  return  true;  else  {CR();  return
false;};">
<b>Enter Subj. + Verb + Obj. or a simple question, e.g., "why...".
</b><BR>
<INPUT TYPE="TEXT" NAME="ear" value="" SIZE="80" onKeyDown="Listen()">
</FORM>


<DIV ID="mouth" style="position:static;
 background-color:aqua">
Output of the Artificial Mind will appear here.
</DIV>


<DIV ID="brain" style="position:static;
 background-color:lightgreen">
Informative messages will appear here.
</DIV>


<FIELDSET>
<LEGEND><font color="red"><b>Tutorial AI Mind Control Panel</b></font></LEGEND>
<FORM name="modes">
<INPUT TYPE="CHECKBOX" NAME="cb1" onClick="HCI()"> Transcript or
<INPUT TYPE="CHECKBOX" NAME="cb2" onClick="HCI()"> Troubleshoot
<INPUT  TYPE="CHECKBOX"  NAME="cb3"  onClick="Tutorial()"  CHECKED>
Tutorial
<INPUT TYPE="CHECKBOX" NAME="cb4" onClick="Shutdown();">
 <font color="red"><b>HALT</b></font>
<INPUT TYPE="CHECKBOX" NAME="cb5" onClick="Destroy();"> Terminate<BR>
</FORM>
</FIELDSET>


<NOSCRIPT>
```

```
<P>The Robot AI Mind requires Microsoft Internet Explorer<BR>
with JavaScript enabled.<BR></P></NOSCRIPT>

<SCRIPT Language="JavaScript">
 // The following code activates the INPUT FORM cursor:
 document.forms[0].ear.focus();   // Display blinking cursor.
</SCRIPT>

<DIV ID="teacher" style="position:static;
 background-color:yellow">
There is no warranty for the AI textbook software.
</DIV>

<font color="navy" size="+1"><b><PRE>
   /^^^^^^^^^^\  How A Mind Generates A Thought   /^^^^^^^^^^\
  /     EYE       \ CONCEPTS                      /     EAR       \
 |    _____       |  | | |    _____        |               |
 |  / cat   \!!!!|!!!|!| |  /            \         |               |
 |  / image   \--|--|-+ |  (  Sentence   )---|--------\ |
 |  \ recog   /   |   |c| |    _____/         |               | |
 |   _____/     |   |a| |       |  \   _____      |   auditory  | |
 | recognition    |   |t| |       |   \/ Verb \      |             | |
 | of a cat       |   |s|e|        |   ( Phrase )     |   memory    | |
 | initiates      |   | |a|     __V__  /_____/      |             | |
 | spreading      |  f| |t| / Noun \/     |          |   channel   | |
 | activation     |  i| | | ( Phrase )    |          |   _____   | |
 |     _____     |  s| | | _____/     _V_____     | /         \ | |
 |  / new    \    |  h|_|_|      |      /English\ | /   "cats"   \| |
 |  / percept \   |  /     \   __V____  \ Verbs /-|-\   "eat"   /  |
 |  \ engram  /--|-\ Psi /-/ Nouns \  \_____/  |  \ "fish" /    |
 |   _____/     |   \__/   _____/------|--_____/     |</PRE>
</b></font>
```

```
<DIV ID="souvenir" style="position:static; WIDTH:640;
 background-color:lightyellow">
MSIE/ View/ Source:   File/ Save As... C:\mind.html
</DIV>

<DIV ID="tabula" style="position:static; WIDTH:640;
 background-color:aqua">
Unclick Troubleshoot prior to clicking on Transcript.
</DIV>

<!— The Troubleshoot columns are present but invisible. —>
<DIV ID="psicolumn" style="position:absolute; LEFT:10; TOP:700;
WIDTH:200; HEIGHT:140; background-color:clear">
</DIV>

<DIV ID="encolumn" style="position:absolute; LEFT:220; TOP:700;
WIDTH:200; HEIGHT:140; background-color:clear">
</DIV>

<DIV ID="audcolumn" style="position:absolute; LEFT:430; TOP:700;
WIDTH:200; HEIGHT:140; background-color:clear">
</DIV>

</body><!— comments of the HTML variety:
Mon. "12aug02A.html" renames "Ruminate()" as new "SVO()" module.
Sun. "27oct02A.html" changes variable "question" to "questype";
streamlines aLife module by uncommenting and calling stubs.
  (end of HTML comments) —>
</html>
```

0-595-25922-7